533
days

Also by Cees Nooteboom in English translation

FICTION

Rituals

Philip and the Others

The Following Story

The Knight Has Died

A Song of Truth and Semblance

Mokusei

All Souls' Day

Lost Paradise

The Foxes Come at Night

NON-FICTION

Roads to Santiago

Nomad's Hotel

Roads to Berlin

Letters to Poseidon

Venice

POETRY

Self-portrait of an Other

Cees Nooteboom

533
days

Translated from the Dutch by
Laura Watkinson

A MARGELLOS
WORLD REPUBLIC OF LETTERS BOOK

Yale UNIVERSITY PRESS | NEW HAVEN & LONDON

The Margellos World Republic of Letters is dedicated to making literary works
from around the globe available in English through translation. It brings to the
English-speaking world the work of leading poets, novelists, essayists, philosophers,
and playwrights from Europe, Latin America, Africa, Asia, and the Middle East
to stimulate international discourse and creative exchange.

This publication has been made possible with financial support
from the Dutch Foundation for Literature.

N ederlands
N letterenfonds
dutch foundation
for literature

First published as *533: Een dagenboek* by De Bezige Bij, Amsterdam, in 2016.
First published in Great Britain in 2021 as *533: A Book of Days*
by MacLehose Press, an imprint of Quercus Editions Limited.
First published in the United States in 2022 as *533 Days* by Yale University Press.

Yale University Press books may be purchased in quantity for educational, business,
or promotional use. For information, please e-mail sales.press@yale.edu (U.S. office)
or sales@yaleup.co.uk (U.K. office).

Designed and typeset in Sabon by Libanus Press, Marlborough.
Printed in the United States of America.

Library of Congress Control Number: 2021950221
ISBN 978-0-300-26450-0 (hardcover : alk. paper)

A catalogue record for this book is available from the British Library.

This paper meets the requirements of ANSI/NISO Z39.48-1992
(Permanence of Paper).

10 9 8 7 6 5 4 3 2

1

The flowers of cactuses cannot be compared to other flowers. They look as if they have achieved a victory, and, strange as it might sound, as if they would like to get married, preferably today, but it is not clear to whom. My oldest cactus, who was here when I arrived forty years ago, is made up of contradictions, as if he is all kinds of different ages at once. He has those large leaves, which of course you cannot call leaves, they are more like big, outstretched hands without fingers, oval shapes, green and solid, covered in little prickles, the cliché of the cactus in a Mexican landscape. I know nothing about cactuses. They were the inhabitants here; I am the intruder. They stand in various places, there is a neglected part of the garden behind my studio where they reign supreme. The cactus of contradictions stands in a different spot. On the tip of what will later become a fruit that is known here as *chumba*, and in France as *figue de Barbarie*, there is now, in the summer, a yellow flower. Some leaves – I shall just continue to refer to them as such – are made of dried-out leather, but sometimes in other places they also have little fingers in a bright and vibrant green. If you remove the spikes you can slice them thinly and eat them. They drop their big dead hands, which are surprisingly heavy. When I am gardening, raking up everything that has fallen from the trees after a storm, I pick them up carefully, ideally with gloves. I throw away something that is dead, but as I come closer I see that the plant, a man much bigger than I, appears to have transformed into wood towards his base, dead, dry and heavy, and is growing new little hands on that dead matter. This is what I mean by contradictions, it is as if I were to consist partially of dead matter but at the same time grew new limbs, even though I have no idea exactly how to picture that. What could be an equivalent of that yellow flower?

Last year, after travelling through the Atacama Desert in northern Chile, I decided to plant a number of cactuses in my Spanish garden. There is a garden centre on the other side of the island. When I asked about cactuses, someone pointed me in the direction of an enormous hairy phallic plant that towered above me. There was no way I would get him into my car, but around him stood a small army of everything that the salespeople also identified as cactuses, and there were plenty of them, officers and privates in a wide range of uniforms. Every time I pointed at an entirely different form and asked what this one or that one was called, the answer was invariably "cactus", and now there are half a dozen of them in my garden, or what passes for one. With one exception, they survived the winter, and they are extremely difficult to describe. In his *Zibaldone*, Leopardi says poets should not only imitate nature and describe it perfectly, but that they should do so *in a natural way*. Easier said than done. In no way do they resemble the cactuses who were here already, the original inhabitants. I am going to try to find out their names using the cactus books I have bought, but it is not simple. One is a small, sea-green column of a plant that comes up to my knees. Another splits after about a metre into a few side branches before simply carrying on upwards. But why do I call them branches? It is as if a part of the trunk has taken a side road. And perhaps trunk is not the right word. A cactus that continues its growth sideways too. Xec, who does not know what he or she is called either, claims it can grow to a considerable size. I believe I have seen that shape before, in an advertisement for tequila. But perhaps it was a label on a bottle, and an alcoholic haze clouded my vision. Then there is also a bulbous, rather ungainly bullet from the First World War, divided into segments, with an infinite number of spikes, so the tortoises steer clear of him. Divided into segments – is that the right phrase? How did Humboldt do it? How do you describe an object that is green, which, because of a number – about fourteen of them – of sharp indentations has lost its Euclidean cone form and *stands* there, close to the earth, dangerous and powerful, trying to convey who knows what message because the spikes he has all over are a shade of deep crimson at the top? But, first lesson, I am not allowed to call them spikes, no matter how viciously sharpened they look, and how large they are. A cactus has *spines*. Humboldt naturally considered characteristics, gender, reproductive capabilities, relationships. I do not have the tools to do so, all I have is my *prima vista*, and the poverty of my language. Because when I say "green", what do I mean by that? How many shades of green are there? Just looking at my six new cactuses and wanting to name their colours makes me the master of the adjective.

In any event, I have built a small enclave for them, bordered on one side by an ancient wall of stacked stones, *pared seca*, and on the other by a number of stones of the same kind as in the wall itself, which I have laid on the brown soil as a porous border, to which the tortoises pay no attention. They are, of course, unable to reach any higher than the lowest leaves, but the wounds of their bites are as unpredictable as the shapes of some of the plants themselves. Around the cactuses I have planted other succulents, which in Dutch we call *vetplanten*, fat plants. One of them, one of the many varieties of aeoniums, has deep-black, glossy leaves so beautifully arranged around a centre that you cannot help but believe in symmetry and harmony as intention. The black of the leaves is so intense and in fact sensual that it would be the perfect adornment for the grave of a poetess who died young. And even though I love my tortoises, this morning I saw the old one, a patriarch who has also survived the winters here without me for endless years, trying with all his might to disrupt the harmony of that mathematical symmetry by perversely biting into it with his old man's gums: sacrilege.

But how to punish a tortoise who has much older rights here than I do? As far as I know, tortoises have no annual growth rings, so I have no idea how old he is, and he pays no attention to admonitions either. What I would really like is to observe myself from his perspective, to see how that might look. A sort of immensely tall, moving tower that, if asked clearly enough, can provide water. At the hottest point of the summer, he sometimes comes onto the terrace and nudges my foot. Then I spray water over the stones, which he licks up, slowly and thoroughly. Millimetre by millimetre, like a living bulldozer, he has pushed aside the stones I laid around the plants last year to protect the lowest leaves from his attacks.

Not only do I know little about cactuses, but I also know little about tortoises, although I do think they have some things in common – stubbornness, wilfulness, maybe even the material of which they are made, hard and tough. Shells and spines are repellents, a tortoise's leg feels just like the skin of some cactuses, and my tortoises lay their eggs under the ground, as if they believe that they, too, are plants. They can go for a long time without water, but they know where to find me when they become thirsty. Maybe they think I *am* water. I have yet to solve the secret of cactuses and water, a mystery of too much or too little. I was here until October, and then briefly in December. Jabi, the neighbour, says it has rained a lot this winter. But in deserts, where they come from, it rarely rains, if ever. Here, after an electrical storm last night, the rain came pouring down. The ficus and the fig tree appear to have enjoyed it, their leaves are gleaming. The cactuses are saying nothing, at least nothing I understand.

They show the peculiarity of their shape as if it is their duty, which of course it is. They obey their DNA just as their ancestors have done for an eternity, a book of law that was once written for them and to which they adhere, paragraph for paragraph. Or did they, in a time before memory, write it

Chumba: *the prickly pear, the fruit of the fig cactus.*

themselves, adapting it over the course of endless trials and jurisprudence? They answer such questions with unrelenting silence. Trees sway, bushes bend, wind roars, but cactuses do not engage in such conversations. They are monks, their growth is inaudible; if they make any sound, my ears are not equipped to hear it, their form is their purpose, as Aristotle knew. They probably do not care that I can see them.

2

On the day I arrived, Xec appeared after a couple of hours, with a book about death.

The postman had left it outside, at the mercy of the rain. Xec had saved the book.

Then we discussed his work. He is a negative sculptor, changing the shapes of trees so the garden receives more light. Half a lifetime ago, I planted palms, they came up to my knees. For years I sawed off the dead palm branches myself, until I was no longer able. The trees – there are two of them – too tall, and I too old.

Palm branches, they belong to Palm Sunday, the Sunday before Easter, the entry of Jesus into Jerusalem, people on the roadside waving palm branches. On Palm Sunday the palm branches were blessed, and you were given a little one to take home, a miniature version that did not resemble a real palm branch, because the place where they are attached to the tree, the part you have to saw off, is full of daggers that can give you a nasty wound. In the wintertime, Xec keeps an eye on the garden, a strange amalgam of wilful inhabitants who were waiting for me when I appeared here more than forty years ago. Some of that population has since died out, this is not a mild climate, and a garden without a gardener has a hard time on an island where the wind is a domineering ruler, sometimes raging from the north and bringing the salt of the sea with it. Xec is young and strong, he came with his little daughter, and it is because of the book he brought that I associated him with death that day. It is a book by Canetti, who did not want to die, but that is in itself not enough to associate a gardener with death. It was something else. I asked him why he had not removed the overbearing lilies that always try to push their way in among the aeoniums. That was what we had agreed. Those lilies – I always call them lilies because I do not know their real name – seem to flower when I am not there, and that alone is a reason to dislike them. But how to describe this dislike? You would have to start with the aeoniums themselves, succulents grouped opposite the terrace like a small army, facing the house, the first thing I see as I begin the day. They are a simple people. Bright green leaves, in a beautifully mathematical circular arrangement, sturdy substance, they have earned their right to exist simply by standing there all this time, mostly in isolation. The lilies are intruders, long thin leaves striving upwards, attached to obstinate, determined bulbs that are hard to remove without taking much of the aeonium too. They have cost me half of my back. Xec had promised to take them out when the ground became a little more obliging and I was roaming around on the other side of the world.

In response to my question, Xec lifted a foot. On its sole

was a large black mark that looked like a form of decay, an ill omen. And it was exactly that – he explained that he had had an operation on his foot for skin cancer. The black mark, the lilies, the book by Canetti with that despairing title, that was how the thought of death had slipped in among the cactuses and the tortoises. I thought about Canetti's grave, which I had once visited in Zurich, not far from Joyce's burial place. I went there twice. The first time, like Brodsky in Venice, he had a Catholic cross, which was later replaced by a grave without a cross, but that did not make it a Jewish grave. There were, though, individual pebbles on both graves, as I had seen on Celan's and Joseph Roth's graves in Paris, but the most striking thing about those tombs in Zurich, so close to each other, was the difference in character. Joyce sits there, untroubled, legs loosely crossed, a man on a Sunday morning, who might just as well be smoking a cigarette. Dead people do not usually sit, and they certainly do not smoke. Someone who is sitting can rise, although upon death there will be no resurrection for the time being. That will not come, if it comes at all, until the end of days. With Canetti's, the only decoration was his signature, which had something furious and grim about it, the end of an angry letter to an adversary who was too stupid – that was what it most closely resembled. When I open his book, I read: "The risen suddenly accuse God in all languages: the true Last Judgment." Outrage in this sentence too. Life as a conspiracy against humans, dreamt up by God, a gift with a death sentence thrown in. Earlier in the book he visits the place where he would one day lie, a place he had chosen himself. Then it seems almost like the opposite, like longing. He wonders what Joyce will think of him coming to lie so close. But because Canetti is a man who does not dismiss himself easily, he also wonders how he will like lying near Joyce, about whom he has, after all, written: "If I were entirely honest with myself, I would have to say that I would like to destroy everything Joyce stood for. I am against the *vanity* of Dadaism in literature, which elevates itself above the words. I idolise the intact words." Those are the words of one of the People of the Book, as becomes unmistakable when he continues: "The most essential part of language for me is the *names*. I can attack names and bring them down. I cannot break them into pieces. That applies even to the name of the one I hate most, the inventor and keeper of death: God." Joyce and Dadaism, a thought that had not occurred to me, but hating someone who does not exist could also be a form of Dadaism.

As coincidence would have it (but for readers there is no coincidence), at the same time I am reading an older book by Philip Roth, *Sabbath's Theater*, in which, like Canetti, the protagonist, Mickey Sabbath, goes in search of the place where he wishes to be buried. Two Jewish men looking for their graves, and with Sabbath, too, there is an obsession with death. The book is a frenzied aria of Eros and Thanatos, up to and including his repeated masturbation on the grave of the adulterous woman with whom he had a hyper-erotic relationship, which is depicted extremely explicitly by Roth, the surfeit of details leading to occasional vicarious exhaustion for the reader, as if he had to walk up an endlessly long mountain path in suffocating weather until he can go no further, and for the reader that I am, this is the opposite of eroticism in Nabokov, who can be equally extreme but via suggestion, not through an unstoppable outpouring of wild aberrations and realistic details.

Sabbath, then, is no Humbert Humbert, but in all his grotesque obsession he truly is an unforgettable figure, and it is this figure who wanders around lost in a neglected cemetery in the provinces and negotiates with the superintendent about the where and, in particular, the how much of his burial, a sum he pays on the spot. I do not know if Canetti would have recognised any of this, although the scandalous text that Sabbath wishes to have on his gravestone and which he hands over in a sealed envelope to the cemetery man, together with the money for the funeral and the costs for the rabbi, would have disgusted him. The difference is, of course, that Sabbath did not really exist. Non-existent people need more words, while Canetti was able to suffice with his signature on the gravestone and the names of his first and second wives, Veza and Hera.

3

When is something an event? A train accident, a completely unexpected visit, a lightning strike. Lightning regularly hits this island in the summer, a sky full of electrical *mene tekel* and then a mortal blow. This appears in the local newspaper the following day, an event. What do you call it when something happens that would never count as an event for the outside world, but does for you? Early morning, the *esteras*, a sort of blind made of woven reeds, not yet lowered. I am sitting on the terrace when a hoopoe lands beside me, making a dramatic entrance. He has not seen me, or he would have fled. The *Upupa epops* is very shy. But here he sits, beside me on the dry brown soil, beside the recently planted hibiscus, which refuses to grow. If there is one bird that resembles a flower, it is the hoopoe. In Spanish he is called *abubilla*, here on the island, *puput*. Does he know that he is beautiful? He has a tall crest of upright feathers that start as a cinnamon colour and end in black and white at the top. His long, curved bill is grey brown, his legs slate grey, the tip of his tail a thin strip of white and then a broader band of black. I sit there, perfectly still, but as soon as I move my hand just a little, he is off. I see him, clearly a male, disappearing across the neighbours' field with his strange, low, rising and falling flight.

I have never seen this bird's nest, apparently he makes a huge mess of it, as is sometimes the case with beautiful people. Is it an event if the day is different afterwards?

4

"Il faut cultiver notre jardin," says Voltaire at the end of *Candide*. And what if it were different, or the other way around? I am not a plant, but what if it were the garden that was cultivating *me*? Teaching me unexpected forms of attention? I have never thought about the red of the surfinia before. Maybe I have not even really thought about red itself, or why it is that there are some sorts of red that you would like to call black. The hours of the day, the presence or absence of clouds, bring their own forms of painting. And of theatre. No clouds, the hottest part of the afternoon, the surfinia turns blood red, the red that follows a crime of passion, malicious, the black red in the sand of the arena as the bull is dragged away. A change of wind, *tramontana*, the threat of a storm, ash-grey sky, the surfinia a sudden actor, master of mimicry, lead-coloured black creeps into the red, trouble is brewing, I have been warned.

5

Literary politics (such a thing exists: hegemonies, influences, triumvirates, legacies) and death. Elias Canetti ("The Prophet Elias [Elijah] defeated the Angel of Death. My name is becoming increasingly uncanny to me.") on Thomas Bernhard. He claims him for himself but is afraid he will have to surrender him to Beckett. "I elevate him to my student and of course he is that, in a much deeper sense than Iris Murdoch [his former lover], who changes everything into pleasantness and light and has essentially become a clever and engaging entertainment writer. For that reason alone, she cannot be a real student of mine, because she is obsessed with *sexuality*. Bernhard, on the other hand, is, like me, obsessed with death. Recently, however, he has been under the influence of a man who puts my own in the shade, namely Beckett. Bernhard's hypochondria makes him susceptible to Beckett. He is receptive, vulnerable. Like Beckett, he yields to death, he does not stand up to it. [. . .] So, I think that, because of this reinforcement by Beckett, there is something approaching an overestimation of Bernhard, but an overestimation that comes from above: the Germans have found in him their own Beckett."

A student dismissed serves another master, has put water in the wine of death. Punishment. That was in 1970. Bernhard reacts furiously in *Die Zeit*. Six (!) years later, Canetti writes a letter back to him, which he does not send. "I have criticised you harshly and now you are senselessly lashing out." The last, unsent sentence: "You have no-one who tells you the truth. Does the truth no longer matter to you?" For Canetti, death was an arch-enemy who had to be fought like a living adversary. He hated those who made common cause with the enemy, his hatred was not abstract. Senselessly lashing out, that is something I would like to do too. What is missing from me?

6

Once, over half a century ago, I wrote a book, *The Knight Has Died*.[1] The sound of a night bird reminds me of it. The book is set on a Mediterranean island, not this one, closer to Africa. I hear that bird here too. Back then, I described the repeated sound as *glook*, silence, and then *glook* again. I have not reread the passage, but I recognise the fascination of the sound because it is repeated over and over as if indicated by a metronome, the intervals are always the same length, you can count along. The bird book gives the sound of the Eurasian scops owl as *chuh*. That end without a sharp consonant is correct –

1 Translated into English by Adrienne Dixon.

actually, a softly pronounced *pooh* would be the best imitation. It is a very mysterious sound, and if you listen closely you will hear the response, which sounds the same, but quieter, a sound that belongs to the night, and to the hunt, a call that heralds the death of bugs, beetles and spiders. He calls, she responds. I am drawn into an invisible intimacy, hidden in the darkness of the Mediterranean night.

7

Between the world of the house and the world outside, I have a Menorcan gate, made from the wood of the wild olive, which is first dried, then placed in water and forced into a particular shape, six or seven slender, slightly curved cross branches, unpainted and long, and across them a single one, angled from top to bottom, the final piece that holds everything together. The men who make these *barreras* are called *arraders*. In the past they used to travel from *lloc* to *lloc*, the farms where there was always something or other to repair. They are the last, along with the wall builders. Out in the countryside you still see their gates, although these are giving way to tall painted barriers that you can no longer look through. Often it is the houses of people who are not from the island that lie behind them, the height of the gates and the invisibility of the life going on behind them indicating both possession and the fear of losing it. *Barrera* is the name of my gate, it has no lock and therefore no key, you close it by putting a long metal hook through a ring, but usually we do not, and you open it by taking hold of the uppermost bent branch, but when I tried to do that this week, a moth the size of a child's hand was sitting there. No doubt about it, a creature of shameless beauty, a design by the Wiener Schule, efficient, plain, monastic, severe in a modern way. Its colour was that of the dried wood, the perfect camouflage. He or she was not sitting there for no reason and, whichever gender it was, the creature did not remain alone for long. From that moment on, there were two of them, a friendly married couple. I was happy they had chosen my gate. I did not have to protect them – they were too big for the geckos that live here, rats do not climb up gates, and falcons, owls and buzzards do not come that close. Their greatest enemy was me, but we did not know that at the time. From that first, surprising moment, I saw them almost every day. Usually they flew off when I wanted to go through the gate, but they were seemingly so tame that Simone could photograph one quite calmly. With that photograph in my hand, I looked through my butterfly book, as moths fall under butterflies, at least in the Spanish book I have here. But I could not find him. I saw the strangest designs, Gucci, Armani, models of great beauty. I understand that some people would rather believe in God than in the Big Bang and the ensuing eternal great Course of Events. As I happen to live in a world of designers and artists, there always has to be a signature somewhere, although we have never seen God's, unless it is that very moth. Moth or butterfly, that is the question. From what I had learned, the vision of elegance in our photograph was a moth, but which one? Did he have no name? Why was he not in the book? The dénouement – and the disillusion – came today. Under a pile of old newspapers we found a warning

Oruga barrenadora de las palmeras

from the island council, left here from last year. *ALERTA!!
Your palms are at risk!* I remembered that Xec had told us he
had injected the palms with some substance or other because
there was a creature that threatened palms in particular, just
as a few years ago we had had to combat the processionary
caterpillar plague by hanging something in the pine trees. So
now it was the *Oruga barrenadora de las palmeras* that had
to be fought off. I also understood why I had never found him
in the butterfly guide, my book was from 1985 and he was
a recent immigrant, a predatory invader from Uruguay and
Argentina, who was after our palms. Now I could see him
properly for the first time, because in our photograph he had
closed his overcoat over the part of his attire that would have
enabled me to recognise him. In the photograph in the leaflet
his wings were spread wide, so that his undergarment was
visible, and it was that piece of clothing that gave him away,
a composition of black and orange with, in the middle, vigor-
ously applied patches of white, opulence under the monk's
habit, a dangerous saint. I took a closer look at the photograph. I do not know what the different parts of a butterfly are
technically called. Head is head, that much is clear, but what
I call an undergarment is perhaps called a rear wing. Simone
had taken the photograph from above. Two feelers that are
actually called antennae, a carapace, two lateral limbs. The
carapace suddenly made him look like some kind of street-
fighter. It ended a little frivolously with, on the left and right,
something that looked like hair. The wings, still stretched
down in that photograph, were various shades of brown and
light brown, becoming paler in colour towards the middle,

with two small angled bands of white as an ornament, a sort of officer's insignia. Half of the body was visible, it had black rings or bands, and was made of some unpleasant material that, as with many insects, was reminiscent of the sinister armed enemy in a science-fiction film. There are forms of beauty that, when magnified, can become part of the arsenal of the nightmare. Also, he had suddenly become an enemy, but how do you kill a butterfly? I planted those palms more than thirty years ago, and they are close family. His beauty has proved fatal to him today. We had thought him beautiful and had become accustomed to him, as an unexpected gift that belonged with us. A new friend of the household, whom we would never have chased away. And that love was mutual. That was why he always sat with her – or she with him? – on our gate. But not anymore.

We caught him – and drowned him. He flapped his wings a few times, but between two forms of betrayal I had to choose the lesser. In the leaflet from the island council (*Departament d'Economia, Medi ambient i Caça*), I had seen the same kind of photographs as on cigarette packets – damaged lungs here, palm branches slumped in mourning there. Science calls him *Paysandisia archon* (Burmeister, 1880). According to my Greek dictionary, an *archos* is a leader, ruler, commander. And *archon* would be the accusative form. Today that was true. It was all about accusation. The only consolation is that butter-flies do not usually live for long, most measuring their time in days, sometimes weeks, but that is it. I have learned that there is little to be said about the mystery of time and duration.

Now that I knew what he was called I could set off into the

internet, which always leads to side paths and detours. As is often the case these days, he was probably a she, the females of the Castniidae family are usually larger than the males, and you can easily mistake them for a butterfly. Wing width of up to 110 millimetres. The larva, which is white and looks like a maggot, eats away at the roots and trunks of palms. Death had flown into my garden in the form of a jewel. And as I was travelling along one of those many side paths, I found another fairy-tale figure, the egg of the comma, *Polygonia c-album*, who also does not appear among the two thousand species in my Spanish book of butterflies. I am a lost explorer and all I find is strangers. I have no idea how many times the photograph has been enlarged. "The egg on the left has already hatched, but the one on the right has not," it says. But how is it possible that the egg on the right looks like one of the cactuses I planted last year? A large spherical green egg, with a form as regular as a sonnet, but covered in angry spines.

For readers, there is no coincidence, as I have already said. Today I received a book from a South Tyrolean poet friend, Oswald Egger. It is called *Euer Lenz* and has nothing to do with butterfly eggs or cactuses, and yet I think there is a connection, though in order to prove it I will have to read the book for another year – I think this because I heard Eggers give a reading a few months ago, and because I looked first at the illustrations and read the captions. Alongside a pale photograph of something that looks like a relief carved in wax, it says: "Wie die Rinde der berindeten, dünnästigen Birken birst, bin ich – *Bostrichus typographus*." I don't know whether it is correct, but I translate the line into my own language as "Zoals de bast van de omschorste duntakkige berk barst, ben ik – *Bostrichus typographus*", "As the bark of the bark-covered thin-branched birch bursts, I am – *Bostrichus typographus*" – and when I look back at the picture, I see a psychogram intended as a self-portrait. The second illustration is a dark Charles Darwin, not a portrait of the scholar, more an etching or engraving by his hand of something that resembles an upright structured molehill: "Die Bildung der Ackererde durch die Thätigkeit der Würmer. Stuttgart 1882." (The Formation of Vegetable Mould through the Action of Worms). And the third illustration shows a boy lying on the ground with his legs up to form a letter Y, and beneath it a quote from Eichendorff: "I want to go out into the world like a desperate man, want to stand, like Don Quixote, on my head in the mountains and be really insane for once." I have wanted to do so all my life, I add, and a man who believes windmills are giants may also see a butterfly's egg as a cactus. On the eternal detour, the pilgrim must measure out his insanity in order to be able to cope with it.

Did I understand Egger's poems when I heard them, that evening in Düsseldorf?

I do not believe I did, because when I read them now, here in the silence, without an audience around me, and without the poet, much still remains unclear. But like then, it hardly matters. Some poets have that, a druidic singsong that tells you what you are hearing is fine. You allow yourself to be rocked along on a voice and a rhythm because you know that voice belongs to someone who is absolutely sure of himself and who is in his own universe. You trust the tune, you have sent your reason away to rest on a park bench somewhere, this language wants first to be heard. When Lucebert read, too, you heard the poem long before you understood it. Witchcraft, a form of enchantment.

8

A walk in the north of the island, where it is rough and stony. There is a narrow path, said to be a thousand years old, running along the coast, following the shape of the island. It is called the Horse Path, Camí de Cavalls. It was towards evening. The coast is elevated there, high cliffs descending steeply, when you get closer to the edge you hear the sea arguing with the rocks far below. I walk to a pile of stones, when I come closer I see that it is a structure, the stones piled roughly on top of one another, but the entirety has an intended form, a clumsy monument. When I walk around it, I see on the back, facing the sea, a rectangular plaque with words that are almost impossible to read, something about a ship that once sank deep below. I do not know why that plaque is positioned to face the sea and the north wind, no-one walks behind it. If I had walked on, I would never have seen those words. A general, a semi-obliterated name that means nothing to me. The whole has something heroic about it, the wind that rules here is the *tramontana*, someone wanted to preserve a name and the whip of the wind wants to erase it. Many ships have perished here. Around me, thistles reaching almost to my waist, leaves of rusty iron. In the distance, a group of horses, about five of them and a foal. They have lifted their heads, they have already heard me, I am the only person here. They stand very still, as do I, we look at each other, I am their event, they are mine. Together we hear the sound of the surf below. Maybe there are some goats or sheep somewhere too, people have used the stones lying all over to make strange round structures with low openings, where animals can take refuge in bad weather when storms sweep across the land. They look like the remains of a lost civilisation. And then I hear the gulls. There are many kinds of gulls, the ones here speak a different language from the gulls on the canal at home in Amsterdam. Sometimes they sound like whining children, an obscene giggling, then a strange cackling as if they are laughing at someone, the odd whinnying laughter of old men or the sound of Macbeth's witches' wicked chanting. I stand and listen, and without warning, I think about my father, who has been dead for seventy years now. A memory so absurd I can hardly believe it really happened, but when I close my eyes I see it. My parents were divorced, I was living in The Hague with my father and his new wife. It was the winter we call the Hunger Winter, just before I was to be sent to my mother in the countryside. Later that same winter, at the beginning of March 1945, my father would die in the bombing of the Bezuidenhout neighbourhood. In the lorry I was allowed to ride in, someone gave me bread and butter and I immediately became horribly ill. The image I see was summoned by those gulls, *mémoire involontaire*, Proust, rather than Nabokov's forceful imperative, I demanded nothing of Memory. My father is kneeling on a flat zinc roof. He has built a frame from four narrow planks, as if for a painting, but it is not a painting inside that frame, it is an old thin blanket. My father is on a seagull hunt. Can you eat gulls? There is no-one left for me to ask, not my father and not his much younger wife, who emigrated to Australia after his death and after the war and whom I never saw again. She is dead too. Everyone knows about the tulip bulbs, but seagulls? The idea was that a gull would land on the roof, and that my father would drop his construction, but this is where my memory fails me. My imagination conjures up a desperate flapping under the blanket and my father striking, but perhaps I had already fled by that point. And how do you kill a seagull? There is an apocryphal proof of God's existence by Borges. A flock of birds, someone saw them, but how many were there? He does not remember, was unable to count them, knows only that it was a number. So how many were there?

There must be someone who knows, and because no-one knows, that someone can only be God. It does not sound like a proof to me. But still, did my father catch seagulls or not? I listen to the seagulls above me, they sway in circles against the wind, writing a slow and jagged design in the sky, a formula that perhaps means something, but which I cannot read because I do not know the code. When I hear them laughing high above me, I think they know the secret, but they keep it to themselves up there in the domain of the wind.

9

For the past few days, I have been reading Witold Gombrowicz's *Cosmos*, a story in which the man who tells it is called Witold, just as Marcel in *À la recherche du temps perdu* shares the first name of the writer Proust. That is where the comparison ends. The *Recherche* is long but clear, *Cosmos* is short but dark, a paranoid account, described by the author himself as a detective novel. What the book does not have in common with that genre is a solution, because there is none. It ends in the same confusion with which it begins, and the reader that I am has the sense of having wandered for days in an insane twilight world, a forest of obsessions, magnifications, exaggerations, hysteria, microscopic observations related to mouths and hands, secret desires (spitting in mouths, hanging), an exhausting journey through the brain of a writer who wants to write, in his own words, "a novel about a reality that is creating itself [...] a detective novel". In his diary, he writes in 1966: "I am taking two starting points, two anomalies that are far from each other: a. a hanged sparrow; b. the association of Katasia's mouth with Lena's mouth." Katasia is the housekeeper whose mouth has been injured and deformed in an accident, Lena the daughter of the family from whom Witold and his friend Fuks ("red hair, fish eyes") have rented a room in the countryside just after finding a sparrow hanging on a wire somewhere in a forest, a sparrow that keeps coming back in a litany-like repetition of words, lending the story a mesmerising obsessive-compulsive tone, erotic in the sense that the narrator constantly sees connections between the two mouths.

After the sparrow, a cat is strangled and strung up, but at

least Witold does that himself, so there can be no misunderstanding for the reader, even though no-one else within the book knows. Until the end of the book, the identity of the person who hanged the sparrow remains vague, as does the death of Lena's husband, Ludwik, also hanged. What we do know is that Witold, when he finds Ludwik's body, puts his finger in its mouth, and then wipes it on his handkerchief. Of the many erotically perverse suggestions in the book, this one is at least carried out. No, this does not become a real detective novel, the figures are sketched as caricatures and use mannered language with plenty of diminutives (Leon, the man of the house, an ex-banker), the events are absurd or hysterical, catharsis is lacking . . . and yet, and yet . . . what? Cracks in a ceiling described in such detail that the two detectives, Witold and Fuks, can see clues in them, an arrow indicating the direction in which to search, pebbles, blades of grass, everything seems to suggest some supernatural meaning. Not long ago I read somewhere in a nature reserve about a sort of marsh fly that had either twelve eyes or eyes that could look in twelve directions at once because of a certain prismatic formation, which, just as in this book, produced an extreme magnification of a minimal reality, but not one that brings me any closer to a solution. Alongside the words was a photograph of that fly's bulging eyes and, beside that, a photograph of the pond where this clairvoyant insect apparently lived; its eyes were monstrous yet fascinating, a sort of convex gleaming honeycomb that would allow you to see into every back street of the universe.

Something similar is going on with Gombrowicz. You could, of course, keep it simple and talk about a farce with eleven people who, within the story, go on a journey together and meet a priest along the way, but it would be a sinister farce with three deaths: a sparrow, a cat and Ludwik. Or you could talk about a dream, a nightmare, a phantasmagoria, but that is at odds with the intention of the writer, who is looking for a way out, an order, a *form* in all of that, clarity in the chaos surrounding us. No wonder he asks in his diary: "Is reality obsessive by its very essence? In light of our building our worlds through associating phenomena, I would not be surprised if at the primal beginning of all time, there was a *double association*. It indicates direction in chaos and is the beginning of order. In consciousness there is something like its being its own trap."

If that was what he wanted to prove with *Cosmos*, then he succeeded in any case, it is a book like a trap, as are, in fact, all of his books. There is something in them that remains just out of reach for the reader. I first read him in the early 1960s, although I have my doubts about what I might have understood back then. *Ferdydurke*, *Pornographie*. From that last book, I took an epigraph for my own strange book *The Knight Has Died*, which, as it should be, was both maligned (J.J. Oversteegen, *Merlyn*) and praised (Van der Hoogt Prize). The truth, in my opinion, lay in the middle. *The Knight* is an emotional book, in which I tried to free myself of my former romantic self, manifest in a novel written in complete innocence in 1954 (*Philip and the Others*, published in Dutch in 1955 and in English in 1988),[2] although I did not realise that

2 Translated by Adrienne Dixon.

until later. I did this in a rather radical way, by having a writer commit suicide, probably so I would not have to do so myself. After that, I did not write fiction for another seventeen years, because I had realised I had not yet lived enough to do so. What appealed to me about Gombrowicz was the complete lack of compromise and its equally complete otherness. No-one else wrote like that. Meaningless plots and yet a story, detailed and magically written mental confusion that is not couched in a confused way. (*Cosmos*, too, is beautifully written, although I would find it impossible to retell the story, or, as Gombrowicz himself says in the book: "a cloud of objects and matters undeciphered, first one detail then another would link up, dovetail, but then other connections would immediately evolve, other connections – this is what I lived by, as if I were not living, chaos, a pile of garbage, a slurry – I was putting my hand inside a sack of garbage, pulling out whatever turned up, looking to see if it would be suitable for the construction of . . . my little home . . . that was acquiring, poor thing, fantastic shapes . . . and so on without end . . .")

In a literary world that demands *stories*, that is of course an impossible starting point. I no longer remember exactly when it was, but around the same time I travelled to London because I knew Borges, the other writer I greatly admired, would be speaking there, at Westminster Hall. I had first read him in Roger Caillois' La Croix du Sud collection, books with yellow covers. I bought that book, *Ficciones*, in 1956. As far as I know, nothing by him had been translated into Dutch at that point. The blind magician sat far away on the stage, and although I certainly do not remember everything he said, he spoke out of his own universe in a restrained, lightly accented English, quoting from memory, the words pouring out of him, as he spoke about De Quincey, about Kipling, Léon Bloy, H.G. Wells, but perhaps that is not true at all and I only think it because I read so much by him later. During the break we were allowed to ask questions, which we had to write on a piece of paper. I should have known better, but I asked on my piece of paper what he thought of Gombrowicz. If I had read them or understood them better, I would have known those gentlemen were not destined for each other.

I knew they lived in the same city, and I thought perhaps they knew each other. They did, but it was not a success. I did not receive an answer to my question. But how could I ever have come up with it? On the one hand, a dirt-poor avant-garde Polish member of the upper classes, who had happened to be in Buenos Aires when the war broke out in Europe and so could not return. His world had been broken off behind him, Poland was occupied. In that strange city, he had to learn Spanish and earn his money at a Polish bank, a writer still completely unknown in Argentina, who spent his time playing chess at flagrantly homosexual bars. And on the other hand, the classical, canonical master, who lived with his mother, and director of the National Library until Perón said he was no longer allowed to be. One of the biggest mistakes readers can make is to think that the writers they love also love the same writers they themselves admire. A Freudian psychiatrist who is an admirer of Nabokov has to endure Nabokov insulting his hero as a "Viennese quack", just as a Thomas Mann enthusiast has to accept that Mann could find no mercy in Nabokov's eyes. But two venomous remarks from the blind sage in the diary Bioy Casares kept for years reveal that Borges was aware of Gombrowicz, and also make it clear that Borges did not always hover high above the face of the waters but could also come across as a bitchy queen. Gossip is the spiteful stepchild of all literature – the blind poet talks about the "pederastic count" (*el conde pederasta*), about a "scribbler" (*escritorzuelo*) who had dared to recite a poem at a literary gathering and had said that, if no-one stood up within five minutes to come to the front with a poem of their own, they would have to acknowledge that he, Gombrowicz, was the greatest poet in Buenos Aires. That poem was as follows:

Chip Chip llamo a la chiva

and Bioy Casares (or Borges) notes: "Scherzo, not without irony, because *chip chip* is used to call chickens." The poem then continues:

mientras copiaba al viejo rico

and the commentary: "(Descriptive section. This does not mean 'I copied the rich old man', but 'I typed what the rich old man dictated').

Oh rey de Inglaterra ¡viva!

(Castanets. Patriotic exaltation.)

El nombre de tu esposo es Federico.

(Aristotelian dénouement)." The text then continues: "Córdova Iturburu tried to read something, but could not find his papers, whereupon Gombrowicz declared himself the king of the poets. The husband of Wally Zenner, a radical from FORJA, was shaking with fury and was about to intervene."

All of this happened on 22 July 1956. The gentlemen had certainly had fun, at least. But in 1982, Borges is more unpleasant: "It is astonishing (*asombroso*) how some unreadable writers fool (*engañan*) people who are more complex and intelligent than themselves. The cult of Lautréamont has declined, but in Europe they speak seriously about Gombrowicz."

And here the evening reader sits on an island where the fantastical diaries of the maligned count lie in his study beside *The Library of Babel*, collected by the unassailable other, and as you do, completely illogically, I cannot help but think of the last sentence of *Cosmos*, when Witold says he is back home with his detested parents and without any transition adds: "Today we had chicken ragout for lunch." A sentence that fits perfectly in my collection of last sentences, alongside that unforgettable sentence of Vestdijk's (from *De redding van Fré Bolderhey*): "Because when umbrellas are in charge, incomprehension has all but become a virtue."

The translation shows that the poem was not destined for immortality: "Chip chip, I call the goat / as I typed out the words of the rich old man / Oh, long live the King of England / Your husband's name is Federico." The only curious thing is that Borges apparently still knew it by heart. In Bioy Casares' more than six hundred pages of Borgesiana, Gombrowicz is mentioned only twice.

10

Ach, writers and writers. Mulisch, once, out of the blue, to me: "That Slauerhoff, who still reads him these days?"

"I do, Harry." End of conversation.

And later, one time at Arti et Amicitiae: "In thirty years' time no-one will be reading Borges." More than twenty of those thirty have since passed.

Writers nowadays had better not think about posterity.

That is for others to do.

Today, the first figs, more than last year. And a few bunches of grapes on the ancient vine that grows, lonely, on a wall opposite the house. Bright green the grapes, gleaming. An old farmer used to live across the road there, as gnarled as the grapevine, his body just as twisted, forced by hard work into a crooked shape. That was more than forty years ago, he must be long dead by now. His daughter was getting married, so before he left he sold me a small piece of land on which nothing may ever be built. The lemon tree that stood on it has died of old age, but the fig tree still grows every year. I do not need to water him, he endures my lengthy absences and takes care of himself. And when he thinks I have stayed away too long, he throws his figs onto the ground. And then the pigeons who make their nests in the pine trees laugh. But pigeons do not laugh.

11

"Nature is bored to death." Another of Mulisch's sentences. This happens with dead people you have known. They go on talking. It was a real Mulisch sentence, too. You did not have to agree, and he was not interested in that. He had said it, and it meant something. When I then replied that, with that one sentence, he had made an entire German repertoire (Schubert, Schumann, Wolf etc.) redundant, all those emotional Lieder, in which the singer identifies with nature and knows what the stream and the tree are feeling – in short, the poetry of human emotions projected onto nature – then he laughed. And of course it is true that nature feels nothing, as every positivist knows. Nature cannot threaten, a stream cannot think, roses cannot despair. When Albert Samain writes "des roses! Des roses encore!/Je les adore à la souffrance. Elles ont la sombre attirance/des choses qui donnent la mort," these are not lines that any rose would lose sleep over. Roses, Harry would probably say, simply *are*, they have nothing more to do than that, above all they have no need to concern themselves with us and our feelings. I do not know if that is what Gertrude Stein meant by "a rose is a rose is a rose". The philosopher from Königsberg had previously explained that we always remain on the outside of things and can never get through to their essence, a knowledge Kleist found hard to bear. And yet, I also know that once, more than sixty years ago now, I read those lines by Samain in Arles and I still know them by heart. Now that we know all the laws, it is easy enough to put romantic misunderstandings in their place, to strip down myths and stories, but then things do become rather bare. Here, by the sea, you can still read the constellations to which the Greeks gave the names of people and animals, groups of stars that also allowed the Phoenicians to find their way to this island by looking at the sky, a place where the moods of the sea, the whims of the wind, the absence or presence of the moon never leave you untouched, even now. So was Mulisch wrong? No, of course not. And yet, there was a curious contradiction in his one-liner, because he, too, was attributing a sentiment to nature. Boredom is a human state of mind, and one with a great creative effect. *Langeweile*, it is almost onomatopoeic, as is the name of the man who wrote about it in such detail, Heidegger, only in that case I do not know what it might be. I know boredom as a requirement for writing, it is a part of travelling, just as it is of country life, perhaps that is what Mulisch meant. Animals do not suffer from it, even though they, too, become restless here when the *tramontana* blows, particularly when it goes on for days. People here used to jump into a well in the winter if it went on for more than a week. One of the villages in the middle of the island apparently had – or still has – the highest suicide rate in Spain, and even if that is not true, you can feel it when you walk its streets, a gloomy Arab village. When the rains begin, I like to go there for a drink.

This is an island of the wind. Suddenly, in the middle of the perfectly silent night, it is there. The noise wakes you up. Because even though those trees feel nothing, they are moved, and that moves us, or at least me. Something Roland Holst would have called a great blowing. An intense murmur, swelling. A palm tree rustles differently from a pine tree, and the big *bella sombra* that one day will lift up half the garden with its elephant's feet makes a different sound from the wild olive. The composer that is the wind knows that. What I hear at night is an opus without a number. The storm works with sound effects. At first I think it is raining heavily, I get up, go to the balcony, but it is not heavy rain – that does not come until later. And it is always different. Sometimes *sostenuto*, a steady sound, *unisono*, no individual voices. At other times a raging attack, charging into the bedroom at night like a furious drunkard, cracking a whip here and there, screaming, tugging at the curtains and making them flap around like a flag at sea. Or turmoil with silences, as at the beginning of Stockhausen's *Gruppen*, violence alternating with nervous little explosions, later degenerating into a pandemonium, sophisticated aggression that makes you lie still, hold your breath and listen, wondering if the donkey is sheltering somewhere or what the pigeons who make their nests in the pine trees are doing now. Usually it ends in a prolonged *Rauschen*, the word that Heidegger uses in association with boredom, because if you do not flee boredom but surrender to it like a captive, you can hear what Rüdiger Safranski calls the background noise of existence, with all its associated emptiness and fear. But I must not confuse these things. The philosopher's noise is metaphorical, it has nothing to do with my storm, you actually need to hear nothing in order to hear that sound. Boredom is the absence of noise. But when the wind is blowing, I hear all kinds of things, whispering, sighing, hissing, suggestions of danger and violence, and then it is impossible to be bored. The branches of the plumbago, which now in August have so many blue flowers, bend backwards like swooning gentlewomen, the hard branches of the palms whip one another, the yucca defends itself with its vicious daggers, the tall papyrus lisps and rustles, the pines, the tallest trees around here, are in a state of great agitation and yet think nothing of it, and the next morning I rake up the needles and the new green tufts, along with everything else that has fallen, including one day a nest of almost embryonic young rats, which the mother rat who lives in one of the walls had placed in the heart of the palm tree, greyish little bodies, still hairless, in a huddle, dead before they had lived. I knew they were there – I had sometimes seen the rat come out of the wall, a lightning-fast shadow, and run across the long, curved palm branch, which reached the wall, and up into the top of the palm tree. And then, the day after, nothing, the silence of a Trappist monastery, the trees motionless, like pillar-saints, immobile. Not a leaf moves. Nothing rustles and nothing falls. All you can hear is the sound of my rake, a wide, fan-shaped instrument with strips of thin and flexible metal, their many tips close together. I gather the needles as if they are gold. Something that was above is now below. When Xec comes, I show him the green ends of the branches – they look like green festoons or gnomes' shaving brushes, but they should still be up there, not on the ground. There are a lot more of them than last year. He breaks one of them in two, at the point where the brush is attached to the branch, and takes a look. Then he hands me the branch and points at something white. I ask if it is a worm but he does not know, neither does he know what it actually is. He collects a few of them, says he will send them to the Consell. They can examine it there, they are the ones who sent out the warning about the palm moth. They know everything. If it is dangerous, they will let me know. I do not see a worm, but the sickly colour and the fatty substance are unsettling. Those trees are family. When I walk back and look up, I feel as if someone is quietly laughing at me.

12

"Nature cannot threaten, a stream cannot think, roses cannot despair," I wrote above, and also "of course it is the case that nature feels nothing, as every positivist knows". My friend Hamish does not agree. He comes from New Zealand, paints flowers, has lived on the island for ever, is an avid botanist with a huge garden, and talks to his plants. But he is also a mathematician, and sees no contradiction there. "No, of course not, they're my companions, and it makes a huge difference if I talk to them. They know that, and when I've been away from the island for too long they let me know about it, they have their ways." He brushes aside the subject of boredom. "They're far too busy for that." He points at my single column-shaped cactus standing perfectly still in the heat, pretending not to hear us. "You have no idea what he's up to," he says. "Surviving?" I venture. "That's the least of it," Hamish says, "how about just *being*? Existing. That in itself in an entire strategy. And, of course, he has a completely different understanding of time."

He must have, I think. Whenever I head his way, he is standing there, to attention, if he had arms they would hang down straight beside his body, little finger on the seam, ready for inspection. He is around half a metre tall, sea green, a few outward-facing seams running vertically up his body, but no matter how hard I have searched in my three books, I cannot find his name. Sometimes we just stand there, looking at each other. It is always hard to talk about these things without a human reference. Boredom. Time. Particularly time. For the past few weeks, there has been a spider at the edge of the bedroom ceiling. Originally it was a low farmhouse attic, where things were probably stored for the winter. The house is not large and does not have a cellar. In order to make it habitable, a bricked-up Romanesque arch between two rooms had to be knocked through and the roof raised. The ceiling, painted the white of a polar sea, now has a pattern of rectangles made by laying nine white-painted rectangular beams beneath another nine thinner beams. The entirety looks like a work of art by Schoonhoven, who, even when he became rich and famous, continued to work at the post office in his hometown of The Hague, selling stamps from behind a counter, because he thought it was better for his concentration. This response had an element of a Zen koan, and it meant something to me. A form of boredom as method. I can look at those so-white rectangles for hours. They create a great sense of order and peace, soothing when you have just returned from the realm of dreams, where it is not always peaceful. In some places, the white rectangles are not as large, but that does not detract from the geometric uniformity; the asymmetry, the imperfection, is the charm.

One morning, I saw the spider. It was suddenly there. I tried to remember the previous, spiderless day, but I could not. Very few insects come into the bedroom, so I wondered why he or she had chosen that place, and how long they would persevere. She reminded me of one of those medieval Dutch nuns who, out of penance or a desire for mystical ecstasy, were walled into their cells, like Sister Bertken from Utrecht. The silence inside such a cell must be deafening. The word boredom no longer applies, but I cannot imagine what you might call the sixty years a woman would voluntarily spend there, or what time might mean in such a life. Every day when I awoke I saw the spider, a nun of the animal kingdom, but that, too, is merely an interpretation. She sat there, perfectly still, day after day. I thought she was going to die of starvation and, with my limited frame of reference, I wondered if she was not bored to death. I understood that she was not fantasising about a possible victim, and yet her motionless, silent waiting posed puzzles I was unable to solve. I, too, had to wait. Again that semantic mouse trap: maybe what that spider was doing up there was not waiting at all. I was the one who was waiting – and only when I saw her.

A few days later I awoke and knew at once that something was happening or, rather, must have happened during the night. From my horizontal position, I had, when I opened my eyes, not seen a web against all that white, but after a while I saw it, at some distance from the black dot another much smaller dot had come along. She must have caught something. I tried to look with binoculars but that only made the dots even more blurred. I got up and walked over to her. The second dot was not a fly, but another, smaller spider, another one with those long thin legs with a kink in them.

Neither of the two was moving. Was it a child, a potential sexual partner, a friend, a companion in misfortune? Or perhaps an enemy? I stared and stared until I saw the web do a sort of little jump, bouncing, the other spider swaying along in thin air. Love? Companionship? Food? Eighty years in this world and no idea about cactuses, spiders, tortoises. I am going to die stupid. For the first few days, the three of us lived in this status quo. Until one day the second dot was gone. Had A eaten B? Had B fled? Where does spiders' excrement go? Out in the wild, this is not an issue, of course, but within the immaculate, clinical framework of a Schoonhoven composition, an ascetic Mondrian without colours, such a thing becomes an essential question. Who did what to whom? In the barely visible web, I saw the tiniest of dots, motes of dust, spider-coloured nanoparticles. Are there, for spiders, parts of other spiders that are inedible? Are spiders cannibals? My spider, A, the one who was there first and so had woven the web in which B had ended up – was she a cannibal? I could ask books those questions, of course, but I did not want to do that yet. Writing lives on secrets. The only option was to go on waiting. If A had eaten B, after first letting her meal wait around nearby for a few days and nights (does that make spiders taste better?), she was probably satiated now, and she could wait in peace (also a human reference) for her next victim. This dilemma was solved by Carmen, who comes to clean the house once a week. I had forgotten to inform her about the new family situation in the bedroom. The next morning, there was no more A and no B. I would have to look out for something else to help me think about time and duration. Cactus years, spider days, human time, Dalí's melting watch.

13

Dreams. For me, that brings two questions to mind. The first: where do we find the people who appear in our dreams, the ones we don't know? How do we form, or to put it differently, create them? Out of what material? At night, are we, in a way that has nothing to do with the physical realm, actually sculptors? The people in our dreams move, sometimes they even speak. That's quite something, but how do we do it? And the second question, suddenly quite urgent to me: where are we when other people dream about us? If we assume that we are in the locations where the dreams of those other people are taking place, then last week I was in Berlin, in Ireland, in Vienna and at a reading in Germany. If, on the other hand, we think that temporarily we really, and not really, exist in the head of the dreamer, then this week I was in Medellín, Colombia, in Washington D.C., in Bad Segeberg in Schleswig-Holstein and perhaps also in Venice. One thing is certain, I had no choice in the matter myself – that is not part of the terms of employment. Others dream of you, and you have no say. Once you are told, there is no escape. Your only freedom, if there is any, lies in the question above. Were you in the dreamer's head or were you where the other person's dream took place? There is no other choice, but whatever the case you were not at home in the bed you got out of this morning. You were, without a ticket or a passport – and without even knowing it – in at least eight different countries. It does not sound very believable, and yet it is true. Forms of non-existent omnipresence, *ubiquitas*. This begins to resemble divine attributes, the realm of the shiver. I do not know if that says something about me or about my attitude towards some other people. And it could be even worse, maybe I carried out dream service in places I know nothing about and in the minds of people I do not even know. But I shall stick to the facts, although "fact" is, in this case, a peculiar category. Last week I received emails from four different people, three friends and a stranger, in which they told me they had dreamed about me. Three were from women – one from my German translator, another from an American writer, and one from a stranger in Germany. In addition, two of those dreams featured horses, one dead, one alive. The first dream, a dream from Colombia, was the most detailed one. The dreamer, a writer friend I knew from before, from Medellín, but had met again this year in Cartagena de Indias, wrote that we were together in Berlin. The email was dated 09.08.2014 12:47 GMT–05.00 and came from Medellín. It begins as follows: "It is half past five in the morning here in Medellín, and I just woke up. I dreamed about you, and I want to tell you about the dream before I forget everything. In general, I don't remember my dreams, but I want to tell you this one because I do remember it. I was in the harbour in Berlin, on a wooden ship, a kind of Spanish galleon with a big hold, more like a large sitting room, dark brown in colour. The boat was about to weigh anchor and travel to the north via Poland. I've never been to Poland, but my plan was to get to know the cities of Katowice and Krakow. (I've just looked at the map and those cities are in the south of Poland, far from any harbour.)

"You came on board and were also planning to go to Poland and the Baltic from Berlin. It seemed a bit strange, but I thought maybe we could get there on this galleon by sailing along canals and rivers. You sat in a chair to watch television, but I didn't want to, because I was talking to one of the sailors to ask if I could bring a grey horse on board, as that seemed a far better way to explore the cities in Poland that I wanted to visit. The conversation was about how much it would cost to transport a horse in that large sitting room. I thought about the food I'd have to take for the horse, and I was also concerned about how the horse would do its business in the sitting room. You went on watching television.

"I asked how long the journey there and back would take, and they told me: three days.

"That sounded like a really long time and I asked if there were couchettes on the boat (that was what I asked, but I don't know if it's the right word) and they told me that there were not, that there was only a cabin for Mr Nooteboom. They showed me your cabin too: it was like the captain's cabin, and it had a big bed with a canopy. It was a magnificent bed, from India.

"I went back to the sitting room, where you were watching

television in that chair, but the chair had turned into a sort of wooden platform, which everyone who was there was now lying down on, watching television, including you. I left the boat and said I thought it would be a better idea to borrow a car from a friend and drive to Poland instead.

"That was all. Not really strange and not interesting either, but because I'm working on a story (a commission) based on some of Mark Twain's dreams, I thought it was curious to dream and to write about your being present in the dream, and in such an important position."

The man who addressed me with Colombian formality is called Héctor Abad. I met him a number of years ago at the Medellín poetry festival, where everything is different from other poetry festivals, if only because a few thousand people are seated in the arena on the opening afternoon. Later during the festival, which lasts almost a week, you read your poems in classrooms or small libraries, which I much prefer. I am a poet for small chambers, the poetry I write does not resonate with a crowd. The encounter took place at his home, a house full of light and books, the house of a writer. Everyone knew his story, with its roots in the time of *violencia*, a terrible period of Colombian history in the 1940s and '50s, and that violence continues to this day, bringing the country to the brink of destruction, an expression that for once is meant literally, a time of abductions and counter-abductions, guerrilla, paramilitary militias and eternal hostages, areas of the jungle where you cannot go, hundreds of thousands of deaths, history written with people's blood, and it's still not over, even though the two sides are now talking to each other in Havana, reconcilable and irreconcilable opponents around a table with the victims, outcome uncertain. One of the victims of that war was Héctor Abad Gomez, the father of the man who had dreamed of me. He was murdered in 1987 by paramilitaries because of his open and repeated criticism of the Colombian regime. At that first meeting, his son gave me a copy of the magnificent, touching book that he had written about his father. In English it is called *Oblivion*, in Spanish the more meaningful *El olvido que seremos*, the oblivion that we will be, and that, with all its negative charge, is exactly what it is about. "And for the sake of remembering, I wear my father's face over mine" is the epigraph by Yehuda Amichai that the writer has given to the book, and the title and the epigraph combine to express the hopelessness of the situation. On one hand, the grief of someone who loved his father very much, on the other hand the hopelessness of human endeavours, the tragedy of the son knowing that the father, the murder, the victims will be forgotten over the course of history, the great and inescapable vanity of the *condition humaine*. On the day of his death, they found on his father's desk a sealed letter with the last piece he had written for the newspaper: "Where does the violence come from?" The next day, that piece was the lead article in *El Mundo*, and it contains the following sentence: "There is so much poverty in Medellín that you can hire a man to murder someone for two thousand pesos." After the murder, the son had to flee so as not to be murdered himself.

He spent the time after that in Italy as an exile. It was five years before he could return to Colombia, but he had to wait yet more years before he could write the book, which, in spite of everything, is a eulogy, written in memory of his father. Why "in spite of everything"? Because, in his speech at a memorial service three months after the murder, the son said the opposite of what is usually said on such occasions. Here a son says about the death of his father: "I don't think courage is a quality that is passed down through the genes or, worse, even something that can be taught by example. Nor do I think that optimism is inherited or learned. Proof of this is the person speaking to you, son of a brave and optimistic man, yet full of fear and brimming with pessimism. I am going to speak, then, without encouraging those who want to carry on this battle, which, as far as I'm concerned, is lost. You are all here because you have the courage my father had and do not suffer from the feelings of despair and rootlessness that his son does. In you I recognize something I loved and love in my father, something I admire profoundly, but that I have not been able to reproduce in myself and much less to imitate. [. . .] I don't think my defeatist words can have any positive effect. I speak to you with an inertia that reflects the pessimism of reason as well as the pessimism of action. This is an admission of defeat. It would be futile to tell you that in my family we feel we've lost a battle, as rhetoric demands in cases such as this. Not at all. We feel we've lost the war. There is a cliché about our current situation of political violence that needs to be eradicated. This cliché has the persuasive force of an axiom. [. . .] This cliché holds that the current political violence we are suffering in Colombia is blind and senseless. But are we experiencing an amorphous, indiscriminate, mad violence? Quite the contrary.

Murder is currently being used in a methodical, organized, rational way. More than that, if we sketch an ideological portrait of past victims we can gradually outline the precise features of future victims. And there we might be surprised, perhaps, to see our own faces."

He was right about that last point, because the next sentence in the book states with a brief and terrible clarity: "I have to say that all those who spoke that night except me were killed ," and he lists the names. There are four of them.

14

I am now far away from the dream of a Spanish galleon in the non-existent port of Krakow, far from a grey horse on board a ship and a travelling companion inside whose dreaming head I was travelling to Poland while I myself was asleep in Menorca. All at once I am back in the alienating reality of life in Colombia, where I have travelled so much in recent years. Now Héctor Abad can live there once again, and you can move freely almost everywhere in the country, although you have only to read the newspapers to know that victims still fall, even if this is then followed by talks between the various parties in Havana. Some parts of the mountains and the jungle remain no-go areas, and for many Colombians the nightmare and memory of more than sixty years of violence and two hundred thousand victims are not yet over, and neither is the ongoing agitation in the neighbouring country of Venezuela, which when you simplify and summarise everything has the same cause that Héctor's father wrote about: fundamental inequality, developed over the course of history, and thus far no political system has been capable of doing anything about it. Then you have to add in the all-corrupting, ever-growing spectre of drug dealing, crime, violence and counter-violence mixed with politics and revolution.

At the end of his book, Héctor Abad writes about memory and oblivion. He assumes his father's death will also be forgotten and he is not talking in terms of centuries, but decades. Soon, he says, everything will be forgotten. We are, he quotes Borges, already the oblivion that we shall be, and he is well aware that there is little consolation in those words to counterbalance the sacrifice his father made. These are not the words that usually appear on monuments, words, he says, that will gradually decay on a gravestone. In a previous passage, he says he had to wait twenty years to write the book, not to avenge his father's death, but to tell everything, it had to be written down, and he quotes the scene from *Hamlet* that has everything to do with a dream and yet is not one, that moment at night when the ghost of Hamlet's murdered father appears and asks his son not to forget him, to which he, Héctor, like Hamlet, can reply:

Remember thee? Ay, thou poor ghost, while memory holds a seat in this distracted globe. Remember thee? Yea, from the table of my memory I'll wipe away all trivial fond records, all saws of books, all forms, all pressures past, that youth and observation copied there; and thy commandment all alone shall live within the book and volume of my brain, unmix'd with baser matter [. . .]

15

And the other dreams? Have they vanished? My German translator had dreamed about Harry Mulisch and me. She had to organise a literary event with us in Germany, but it could not go ahead because there was a dead horse in the room. Another horse. And Harry is dead – I carried his coffin to the Stadsschouwburg with five friends. Is that why I feel as if I must apologise now for disturbing him? But I have not done anything – it was someone else's dream. And yet, he may not wish to be woken, does not feel like having to perform in a dream with me. The older you become, the more dead people you know, they are nearby, we are surrounded by ghosts. I wrote this in a story, that there comes a moment when you know more dead than living. That is the moment when you yourself enter into the vicinity of death. Had I wanted to meet him, even though it was in someone else's dream? I think so – there is a lot I still have to tell him. Whether he would want to hear it is another question. After each death, the unsaid sentences pile up, wrapped in cobwebs, thoughts preserved and never spoken, memories you carry with you, things done that cannot be undone, which still come knocking at unexpected moments. But perhaps the German dreamer's night was the same night the American writer summoned me to Galway, on the west coast of Ireland. After all, those dreams all took place in one week. How much exercise can a sleeping person take? I could still ask her about it – that is the advantage of the living. I had a memory of long ago, stormy weather, grey, high waves, a long, deserted beach where we looked for wood for the fire in her turf hut. But no, that was not it, she said. I was there, that was all. And I cannot ask the Venice-dream woman anything, because I do not know her. A card with powerful handwriting and no sender's address. I cannot respond to it. Where was I walking? On the Zattere, by the Salute, or across the water again, to the Lido? That is how I would like to see myself, as a sleepwalker on the waves. But I see nothing; they see something. These are parallel lives that are not my own, with which I can do nothing. Time for me to shake off other people's nights. There are already enough mysteries as it is. Why is it that I read, in Spanish, a story by Kafka that is called "Eleven Sons" and then, two days later, receive a letter from Alejandro Zambra in Chile, in which he writes that he based his new novel *Mis Documentos*, which I wrote to him about, on that story by Kafka? Should I have noticed that? Now that I know, I read his book differently, all kinds of different male figures in Santiago de Chile – that, too, now seems like a dream I did not dream myself. I was here all that time, watering my garden, weeding, putting the garden waste in bags that I have to dispose of tomorrow. On Tuesday we are allowed to put them by the roadside. The road to my house is so narrow that the council's bin lorry cannot pass between the stone walls. We have to deposit the bags where the road is paved with tarmac and wide enough to let the lorry through. Xec is coming this afternoon. He has finally received a reply from the Consell. The pine trees need to be sprayed. But they're far too tall, I say. How's that going to work? He laughs down the telephone and says: You'll see. I say that I need to ask him about the yucca, which refuses to bloom, while the neighbours' yucca is full of tall white towers.

16

That yucca is a funny one. It was once given to me, and I do not remember by whom. I shall leave that sentence there, even though it is no longer true. It was Simone who gave him to me, on my fiftieth birthday, as, to my shame, I had forgotten until she subtly reminded me when she read that sentence. Forgetting involves shame, and leaving the sentence there is a form of penance. A yucca has a crown of about thirty long daggers. When I am working in the garden, I have to take care as I come close to him, because he stabs. If I rake my way backwards, he immediately lets me know when I am in his territory.

Long ago, he made it sufficiently clear that I should not get my eyes anywhere near him. The Spanish ending of his name is feminine, but because of all those weapons he carries day and night I have made a man out of him. I do not remember if he developed side branches right away, but I do know he has been here more than thirty-one years and that one of those side branches did not want to grow towards the light. The consequence was a strange construction. That side branch, at a certain point as thick as the trunk, lay along the ground, but because plants seek out the light, he had weakly raised his crown, as a sick man in a wheelchair might do. Since I heard that a winegrower in Montalcino plays Mozart to his vines with miraculous results for the later wine and that Hamish talks his plants into flowering, I sometimes think I can hear them, even though I do not usually understand what they are saying. Except in this case. Though I cannot imagine that my deformed yucca could also have read Goethe, I still heard him one evening whispering something that sounded like "Mehr Licht." There was a Menorcan accent to his German, but the message was unmistakable, and I took a few loose stones from my wall to slide under his horizontal side branch. After just a couple of months, I noticed he was slowly beginning to stand up. I helped by stacking the stones beneath him a little higher, a wobbly equilibrium, particularly when the *tramontana* races across the island.

But it held firm. Last autumn Xec helped me to find two branches and to break them and stick them into the ground in such a way that they form a sort of wedge at the top, which we used to give the yucca extra support. It is working. The whole plant, who looks down on me because he is taller than I am, has four crowns, four tight bundles of sharp knives sticking up into the sky, a breathtaking silhouette, particularly in the late evening. In the summer, a sort of inverted chandelier made of clusters of bright white flowers appears in the middle of each crown, a shining candle of great beauty. The yucca himself remains deformed. Much of the paralysed trunk still lies on the ground, although supported by those two sticks and my stone construction that allow him to raise his crown to the light, but when I run my tape measure along his horizontal trunk, which is in fact just a side branch of the original plant, I see that, if he were to stand upright, he would be considerably taller than the main trunk. So, I have done two things that are at odds with each other: I have a strange invalid on my conscience, and I have saved a plant. Since he said "Mehr Licht" that one time, he has remained as silent as a tree. The daggers gleam and are greener than ever, he stands there in his

The yucca and its daggers

majesty, the fourth crown lower than the others, but he does not bloom. Healthy as a fish, says Xec, which is a strange comparison.

The daggers have never looked as dangerous and menacing. From where he stands, he can look over the walls and see the neighbours' much higher yucca, which does have the white chandelier in his crown, lofty and regal. This makes the fact that mine will not flower something of an affront. According to Xec, this will change, and before autumn, too. I wait, looking at the branch that is still lying on the ground, which does not make it any easier to rake around it, but I also see that my crazy construction, combined with the yucca's willpower and the sunlight, has made him rise upwards at the end of that horizontal branch in a powerful arch, to rival his siblings. To be honest, I had expected more gratitude, but I am not one for revenge, and before my departure I will pile the stack of stones higher, so that my yucca is better able to reach for the sun. This gives my surreal construction the atmosphere of a botanical Laocoön, the priest who warned about the Trojan Horse, and turned out to be right. But because the goddess Athene was biased and wanted to help Odysseus, who had come up with the plan, she sent as punishment two enormous snakes, which wrapped the priest and his two sons in a deadly, suffocating embrace, a gruesome image. Here, one of those snakes lies on the ground, but the goddess has lost her power, the priest is still not dead, and his sons have gained a sister, whom I have nurtured for more than thirty years.

17

Different concerns. Yesterday Xec turned up with Mohammed and a machine. Mohammed is a silent Sancho Panza to Xec's Quixote, who always looks a little as if he is sitting on an invisible horse. I was working in my studio, which is some way from the house, when I heard the sound of digging. I also heard sand or soil falling, and because I was just reading something about Hamlet it made me think about gravediggers and therefore about Yorick. Readers live on references, and referenditis is a serious affliction for readers who are also writers. Xec had a thing on wheels with him, with a reel around which a long pipe was wound. This is not an accurate description. Sancho Mohammed was digging a grave around one of the pine trees, a sort of moat. I was hoping Yorick's skull might appear, but no luck. Xec was reading something in a book that later turned out to be an instruction manual, and I did not dare to disturb them, because Mohammed was leaning forward over his new pit in deep concentration as if indeed planning to find a court jester's skull down there.

It was a rescue operation. After saving the palms from the evil moth from Uruguay, which is doing serious damage on the islands, Xec had now received a response from the Consell – the dangerous white stuff we had seen when he broke off the new, green tip of the pine branch was indeed a threat that could only be held off by inoculating the roots of the four pine trees with a sort of penicillin for trees. This involved exposing and injecting the top part of the roots. On my way to the house, I go first past the four trees with their moat, then the two palms, which may or may not have the fatal moth cancer, and only then past the yucca I cured by my own efforts. An elderly cousin who has been visiting this island for fifty years looked at the garden one night and said, "This garden – it's a portrait of your soul." Eaten away at by moths, with damaged roots and with stones to lift it towards the light – that is my soul. Dorian Gray is nothing in comparison.

18

Five o'clock in the morning. A restless night because of fireworks and music from the village, the end of the fiestas, in late August every year. The night is cool and inconceivably clear. I have no lights on, and above and to the left of the palms I see Orion, my patron saint. Sirius the dog sparkles at his feet, the heavens are so full that I lose my way, partly because I cannot look 360 degrees all around me, but for the night sailors out at sea that same sky must be as clear as a map. I sit on the terrace for a while, listening to nothing. This is the first morning of September, the scent of the damp soil the first indication of autumn. In an hour's time, the morning concert that usually wakes me: roosters, dogs, pigeons, geese, goats, the donkey bearing the weight of the world or experiencing ecstatic joy, who can say? I do not know his language, all I know is that at indeterminate moments he tears the night apart with his unrelenting pathos, after which nothing is the same. Only the roosters reach his volume, their high triumph cutting through the murmuring and muttering of their female companions, or at least that is how it sounds. The geese and goats are further away, a distant neighbour I do not know. Those geese still have orders to guard the Capitol, and the young goats wail with high, thin bleats. The donkey and the nearest roosters and hens belong to Miguel, the wall builder who lives next door. The other roosters call to one another from all sides, a large circle in the vanishing night. It is, all in all, not a cacophony, and yet the composition works with dissonant notes coming from choirs arranged behind trees, lonely singers, oppositions, sudden silences and then shrill shouting. As words are my profession, I often hear what they say. This is nonsense, of course – what I mean is that when the sounds have a certain rhythm I hear or invent words for them. There is one rooster, for instance, with a breathtaking Neapolitan tenor, the sound of which I always recognise because it expresses such happiness, an animal satisfaction, as he jubilantly stretches out the syllables of the same brief phrase and then repeats it for a while like some kind of braggart: let's get laid, he cries jubilantly over his hens, walls and fields, as persuasively as the crickets who, at other hours, obsessively repeat their metaphysical doubt: it's not this / it's not that / don't know what – once you have heard them, you can never get those phrases out of your head. The score of the entire work must be so large that no-one could carry it. Somewhere in all those fields and woods around me, a conductor must be wandering around, who knows how to reach them all and is able to combine an ancient harmony and the joy of the new light with the fear that has been endured and the danger of the slowly fading darkness. The evening belongs to the geckos, the owls and the curlews, the morning to various bipeds and quadrupeds, and those who listen in silence are the snakes, the

61

rats, the ants, the lizards, the tortoises, the spiders, who make sounds that no-one hears, and the human beings.

19

The village I belong to on this island is called San Luis, or, as they write it in Catalan, Sant Lluís, named after St Louis, a thirteenth-century king of France. The village itself is small, with low, whitewashed houses and an equally white church, built sometime at the end of the eighteenth century under the brief French occupation by the Duc de Richelieu, when Count de Lannion was governor here, but it covers a large area, extending to the bays and the high cliffs of the island's wild south-eastern coast. The world outside my walls has antique and feudal echoes. The annual fiesta on the name day of the medieval French king is a ritual festival of horses and riders, with ceremonial rules of the sort that might come directly from the French court, the same since time immemorial, as you can see in the hazy photographs in yellowing newspapers from more than a century ago at the public library in Mahón. Every village and every town on the island has these festivals on the name days of their saints, and everyone can ride in them. The horses are trained to tolerate the shrill brass bands and the rousing blare of music, and they look like Arabian worses, tall and black. The feudal character is most evident on the other side of the island, Ciudadela, as that is where the *caixer senyor*, the marquis or the duke, rides in the lead, followed by the Church, in the form of the *caixer capellà*, the priest. Gentlemen, peasants, citizens and a priest, the Church and the world. My Catalan–Spanish dictionary, almost six hundred pages long, gives the word *caixer* as cashier, but that does not solve the puzzle, and neither do most of the words that appear alongside it, such as *caixer pagès* or *caixer batle*, but a *caixer* has been a rider here for an eternity, and the word that follows *caixer* indicates his purpose in the whole. The *caixer fadrí* is the bachelor, the *caixer fabioler* plays the flute, the leader of the procession of horses is the *caixer batle*. This should actually be the mayor, but the mayor of my village once had a serious accident, and so he is unable to ride. In addition to the *caixers*, there are also *cavallers*, which actually means riders as well, and yet there is a difference, because they have no role within the hierarchy. They usually come from other villages and together they form the *qualcada*, the cavalcade, dozens of men in something that most closely resembles a nineteenth-century ceremonial costume: white waistcoat, white bow tie, black tailcoat, white trousers in black boots and a black bicorn hat. In the days leading up to the festival there is great excitement, the village is decorated, barriers are placed everywhere to allow the procession to pass through and to prevent parking, signs with a horse's head hang on the walls, and there is an atmosphere of excited anticipation. Then, on the last Friday before the end of the month, the big day arrives, the *primer toc de fabiol*. The mayor requests the presence of the *caixer fabioler*, the flute player, to accompany the *caixer fadrí*, who is to receive the banner of the patron saint, after which the first note is played on the flute. Then the banner can be hung on the balcony of the town hall by the bachelor-*caixer*, accompanied by the flute player and the mayor and the rider who is standing in for the mayor, together with two heralds, who are called *Sa vessa mos fot*. The festival can begin, but it does not actually start until the following day, when the *caixer pagès*, the farmer rider, decorates his horse (in Menorcan this is *el caixer pagès preparà el seu cavall per les festes*) for the festival with garlands of flowers and bows in its mane and tail.

Then, at half past four, there is the *repicada de campanes i descarràrrega de morterets*, bells ringing and the firing of mortars, followed by the *sortida de la banda de cornets i tambors* and the procession of giants and musicians. Now comes the important moment. The flute player, who is the only one riding a donkey, goes to the square in front of the town hall, where the mayor is waiting to give permission for the ceremony of the *qualcada*, the equestrian procession. The flute player asks if he can go and fetch the bachelor from the other square, and he will then return with him to ask permission for the festivities to begin. They are given the banner, the first notes on the *fabiol* are played, and all the riders line up. I know the tune that is now played by heart, I can sing it as I am writing, a refrain that circles around itself, captivating and constantly repeated, that cuts through you like a knife. To the sound of these notes, the *caixers* and the riders from San Luis who are not *caixers* now proceed to the windmill at the other end of the high street, where the riders from the other villages are waiting, and when they are all assembled they head in a procession to the town hall, opposite the church, where the *caixer batle* receives the *baton de mando*, a sort of general's staff, before riding the thirty metres to the church, where the priest is waiting with his horse to join the procession. And by that point you really do need to be able to ride, because now the people are allowed to join in, which means that all kinds of dancers and daredevils from the crowd line up in front of the horses and try to make them stand on their hind legs, a wild dance at times, as those horses high up above them have to come back down, with their weight and their hooves, and by this time the dancers have drunk a lot of *pomada*, which can be found in large quantities throughout the village, island gin with sweet lemon. The gin is called *xoriguer*, but when I look up that word in my Catalan–Spanish dictionary I find *cernícalo*, and my Spanish–Dutch dictionary says that is a kestrel, or a lout, and in combination with the verb *coger* (to grab, to seize, to take), it means to get drunk, which is done here on a grand scale every year. The dance with the horse becomes less innocent when the dancers have had a few too many and try to fire up the animals. Anyone who cannot ride and keep their horse under control, with those front legs pawing the air, is in trouble. This year there was a fatal accident in Ciudadela for the first time, after which the mayor, although it was not his fault, immediately stepped down, an unprecedented event in Spain. Every year more people from outside come to these festivities, which once, when Menorca was still an island effectively cut off from the rest of the world, was the highpoint of the year for all these villages, both a marriage market and a bright spot in a year of poverty and long winters. You can still feel some of this in the people who live here and in the fact that all kinds of words in their language do not appear in my large Catalan–Spanish dictionary.

Nineteenth-century cookery books are the best source of information about what it was like in those winters, when there was only one boat a week and the people had to live on what they could take from the sea and the hard, dry soil – farmers and fishers, many of whom had never left the island. The modern boat that brings me from Barcelona still takes nine hours to make the journey. I have no idea how long it took back in those days, but something of the isolation of those times can still be seen in the characters of the islanders.

20

I am a great artist. And a mass murderer, an irresistible combination. How else do I make the people in my dreams? Where do they get their faces from? They have cheeks, they have noses, they have eyes. I do not usually dream of people I know – that could be explained, more or less, although I am not sure how. No, those strangers, those previously unseen creatures that sometimes populate my nights, the corridors they walk along, the stairs, railings, walls, the ample or sparse illumination, the cities – built, but by whom? Does that make me an architect too? And where are the cities in which those buildings stand? What kind of moments are those when I succeed in giving them streets and squares, tall buildings with people walking at their feet, people I have made, city and all? How long did it take me to give those people faces, to make them walk, to turn a corner and head towards me? Who are they? I have never seen them before, but in my dreams I see them, I must have made them myself, sculpted them, I have stolen faces, robbed postures, hands that can move, and come up with clothes to dress them in. Their eyes are a colour – where did I get that from? From whom did I steal them? And are they still alive? I'll admit it, I travel a lot, I visit big cities, I go down the steps into the underground, I wait in the queue for security at all kinds of airports, sometimes there are days when I try to count everyone I see but that is impossible. And where do I buy their glasses? How do I know which newspapers they read? And yet they appear, threatening me or wanting to be seduced, exciting me or pursuing me, I hear their footsteps behind me.

How many people do I see in the U-Bahn in Berlin? In the subway in New York? Old men, children, soldiers, nurses, priests, there must be thousands of them in a day, all of them are people who call themselves I, but to whom the I who is me has never spoken. What did I use to make the beings who visit me at night? Is that why I am sometimes so tired? How long does it take to make a person?

Do I take a face from one person, and a crooked back, a threatening stance from another? Is it someone who sat opposite me on the train in Buenos Aires? I must be a master because I can do it all, I make trees, clouds, snowy fields, I give them a world to live in, and because I know my eyes move when I dream, I also know that I really see everything, and if I did not make it, then who did? Do they always live inside my brain, or do I call on them only when I want to or have to dream? Do I make them mimetically, based on the image and likeness of the millions of people I have ever seen or do I compose them myself without those examples, do I hang cheeks on skulls, do I dye their hair, do I make them old, and does that take longer, one wrinkle at a time? Are children easier? How many hours does it take me to make a flaky skin, how long do I take to make breasts, to make lips, how difficult is a menacing expression, how is death involved, how sharp does the knife need to be that is threatening me? What is the relationship between the knife I have sharpened and the intensity of the fear it evokes? And what about me? I look in the mirror often enough, but I have never seen myself in my dreams, not even when I was present. I do not remember ever having been visible, and yet I was there. And how did those other people do it, the ones who said they dreamed about me? Can a person refuse to be dreamed about?

21

Today the first rains in three months. April might be the cruellest month, but September is often the strangest. The hours before the rain comes are unbearable. The hygrometer wants to go over one hundred, but it cannot. It is best to watch how the trees withstand it. They stand perfectly still in that wet, warm fug, saying nothing, refusing all movement, as if they no longer want to breathe. What is needed is a timpani strike, but the timpanist is sick, or the conductor is dead. Birds stay away, all you can do is look at the sky, where the blackness is gathering. And wait. Everything is waiting, you feel that someone somewhere is counting, but you don't know to what number, an end needs to come but you don't know how. And then it happens, these clouds are not made of cloud, they are made of saturated iron, a crazed electrical trail of runes inscribes itself across the blackness, cloud edifices are torn apart, buildings knocked down, the house shakes, the lights go out, the darkness of Golgotha descends upon the land, and then suddenly there is rain as a liberation, but this is a rain that does not fall but stands, cold, vertical, filled with the awareness of its own power, and everything seems to open up, as if the plants and trees want to scream back in relief, and the first thing I see is the small tortoise, whom I have not seen in a long time and who comes trudging through the sudden mud like a little tank, seeking the deepest point, where he can drink what he has been unable to drink for the past three months. A Mediterranean storm is not the same as a storm over the polder and not the same as a tropical downpour, sometimes you see the following day that the storm has moved to another coast or another island, someone is still writing on the horizon, the light flashes and flickers in the distance but you no longer hear anything, all you see is the scribble and scrawl of the illegible script proclaiming disaster or redemption elsewhere. Redemption, in particular, is mysterious. You see the flashes above the sea, but there is no rain where you are. There is no wind, there are not even any clouds, it must be very far away, and yet it is visible, perhaps a ship out there in the distance is having to face that violence, the island's newspaper has a name for every kind of sea, which has to do with different forms of danger or intensity, just as the sea charts mark the wrecks on the coast. So many ships have perished around these islands.

22

The night after the storm, the sky was clear again. I found my usual beacons, the five large stars of Cassiopeia, the large W that arrives with darkness and stands directly over the house, Andromeda's mother is the beginning of the night for me, just as Orion before the dew heralds its end. The human scale is one of astonishing innocence, and by that I am referring particularly to my own, because I realise that I actually think Cassiopeia belongs to the balcony of my house, just as Orion in August always heads for the first palm at around five, before disappearing towards the sea. I admit that I am relating everything to myself. I do not know most of the stars behind the neighbours' house, because I cannot see them. The local land register describes in detail the limited surface area of my piece of ground, but there is nothing in it about the stars that I believe come with it. While I can find Cassiopeia easily on land, because she appears at night above my house, I have difficulty locating her on the celestial map in my book of stars. I have to use the alphabet to find her, and there she is, on page 124, between Carina and Centaurus, even though her real neighbours in our solar system are Andromeda and Cepheus, daughter and father, keeping it in the family. My book of stars is American and spells with a C all the names that we write in Dutch with a K, like actual Greeks. Kepheus was the king of Ethiopia, Kassiopeia was his wife, who had once claimed to be more beautiful than the Nereids, the stunning daughters of the sea god Nereus. That sort of claim is better avoided, because Poseidon, who is nearly always in a bad mood, punished her and sent a hellish monster to ravage the land in the form of a constant storm, a disaster that could only be defused by chaining Cassiopeia's daughter Andromeda to the rocks and sacrificing her to Poseidon's wrath, which is what would have happened if Perseus had not rescued her. Now, as a reward, Perseus is in the firmament, as one of Andromeda's neighbours, but when I look at the map of the stars, this is of little use to him, because Andromeda as a constellation consists of three stars that represent a chained woman, and all three have Arabic names, Sirrah, Mirach and Alamak, her chained head, her hips and her shackled feet. Somewhere to the side of Mirach (on that map) is M31, or the Andromeda Nebula, a huge spiral galaxy, a distance of 2,537,000 light years away. But what does "to the side of" mean? Whoever gave this constellation the name Andromeda cannot have had any clue of the dimensions that the chained girl would assume. Her head has a spectrum that is called B8 and is typical of a helium star, and her waist, which you might imagine as something elegant, is a red giant with a relatively low temperature of 3500 K, while those chained feet are a double star in the contrasting colours of orange and blue. The myth that helped the Phoenician sailor find his way to Carthage has vanished among all those zeroes and light years.

I always see her mother Cassiopeia at night as a reassuring sign of five simple stars, while in reality there are at least six plus a number of star clusters that my eye does not know how to handle, and this is a puzzle that I, like Kant, am unable to solve. I do not actually wish to know. Standing by the sea a few hours later, I see that, like that Phoenician sailor, she is some way further into her daily journey, which is actually mine too, because, as I stand there perfectly still, I am spinning along with her at a speed I can never feel. I also know that if the sky remains clear tonight, Orion will appear in my garden at the appointed time. Everything that is not right on Earth is made good up above, or so it seems. What, in our naivety, we see as signs, as the depiction of stories once dreamed up by people and written down by poets, are in reality lifeless balls of gas or piles of stones, moving away from one another and from us at infinite speed over the course of millions of years, to which we have given names that they themselves do not know.

23

Anyone who constantly hears another language around them sometimes has a tendency to sink more deeply into their own language, like some kind of deep-sea diver. There is a dictionary of my language that was started once upon a time, back in 1864, and was finally completed not long ago. The first time I saw the complete version was at the University of San Diego, an endless number of volumes that seemed to occupy entire metres of shelving. I later bought a second-hand copy for myself. In my house in Amsterdam it stands on the floor – there is nowhere else that can accommodate it. Sometimes I spend hours reading it, and then I do indeed feel as if I am descending into the infinite depths of my language in a bathyscaphe, where words dwell that I have never seen or read before, names of extinct objects, unimagined professions, variants and synonyms that no-one knows anymore, quotes from poems and books that have vanished, to prove that those words or expressions once really lived in a time now gone for good. It is strange there, in those depths. I love saying those lost words out loud, so that they appear to exist at least just one more time, but after a couple of hours you return to a world where they have lost their validity, as if you have arrived in a foreign country with banknotes that have no currency.

I could not bring my endless dictionary to the island, obviously, but I have a dictionary from 1950 here, consisting of almost three thousand densely printed pages, another dictionary that is almost impossible to lift. An island is not the best place for books. Damp is an enemy, its weapon mould. Anyone who spends a lot of time with books knows their moods. They want to be read, they long for the hand to pick them up, for the fingers to turn the pages. If you leave them unused for too long, they become first unhappy – and then angry. This is true of novels, poetry collections, but above all of dictionaries. If they are not used, then the words revolt. In the Netherlands, we call that large dictionary the "Dikke Van Dale", the Thick Van Dale. It is the treasury of our language. My copy was bound in green cloth, the damp air was slowly eating away at it, the salt that the wind brings from the sea doing its destructive work, and it began to fall apart, the hard cover coming loose. When I picked up the book, it acted resentfully, dropping pages that I then had to put in loose at the back. Maybe it longed to return to its former owner, a person I never knew but who had left their bookplate in the front. H.A. Brongers, it stated emphatically. I did not know who that was, and it was, of course, possible that this person had since died wordlessly, or that the book was still furious at this Brongers for having humiliatingly disposed of it for far too little, after which the further shame had really begun, abandoned in a messy second-hand bookshop, then exposed to all sorts of weather on a shelf at the market among other outcasts and subsequently saved by the person who is writing these words. Books have their pride, they know their worth – when you preserve thousands upon thousands of words as a living memory of the language, you have no desire to be touched by all manner of grubby hands at the market on Waterlooplein. The journey to Spain was perhaps a surprise, the new place of residence between a certain Webster, a certain Duden and a bunch of other foreigners with partly the same but still far fewer words was in itself bearable, but when the winter came and they were left alone, the gradual rebellion began, a sort of Twenty Years' War, waged on my side with sticky tape and glue, paste and needle and thread, until Van Dale gave up first and threatened to commit suicide. That was the point when someone told me about a bookbinder who lived somewhere on the island. I took the moribund Van Dale to her in pieces. She would need him for two months, and then she would return him to me alive. As I said farewell, I felt as if my language were being carried out of the house for burial. Dictionaries are not only treasuries, they are also graveyards, accommodating, alongside the living and the recently born, the dead, the lost and those who are gone for good. At the end of his own too brief life, Proust speculated about the life his book would have after him. A hundred years seemed like a lot to him, but he was either too cautious or too coy. Soon he will have been dead for one hundred years, but his book is nowhere near that point. What he perhaps devoted less thought to was the language. Not only books, but also words are mortal, they disappear, moulder away, become ambiguous or take on new meanings. One day my French publisher asked me which language I had read Proust in, and when, slightly offended, I responded, "French, of course," he said, "But that's ridiculous. In French, Proust is still a work of genius, of course, but it's so outdated, with all those antiquarian forms of the *subjonctif*. Since Proust's death, the English have had three new translations. The French should be so lucky. Nothing ages as quickly as style."

Language, words, style. The past hundred years have seen the death of languages I have never heard or read. It has always intrigued me when people die who are the last ones to speak a language. What happens then? What is their last thought? I imagine those words linger above the deceased for a while because they know they will never return to Earth. Thinking also happens in language. What is it like when, for the last time, something is thought in words that will never be heard again? My Van Dale is back, he is here beside me. The bookbinder made a nice box for him, in the same colour as his still-worn green binding. The first word I look up is not chosen entirely at random. It is the word *mot*, "moth", because that creature is still threatening the palms here. Van Dale knows him, a family of very small butterflies with narrow wings (then he has never seen our *Oruga barrenadora*). And at once the riddles begin, as if the cured dictionary now wishes to repay me by proving me right. I know the word *mot* in the sense of "trouble, a tiff", as used in the Jordaan neighbourhood of Amsterdam, but *mot* as the eye of a *kardeel* is lost on me, because I do not know what a *kardeel* is.

It becomes even more mysterious when the sentence continues: *gewoonlijk rond een kous, aan het lijk van een zeil gesplitst*. For me, a *lijk* is a corpse, the body of a dead person, the connection with a *zeil*, normally a sail, is unclear, and a *kous*, a sock or stocking, means nothing to me in this context. So, it is usually found around a stocking, spliced on the corpse of a sail? There are no doubt people for whom these words are still alive, but for me they are dead. This is what I mean by the dictionary as graveyard. Van Dale is pleased. I can feel it. There are no more loose pages, the green cloth fits like a suit of armour around his sizeable body, and he is looking forward to pushing that Webster aside. I take a look at *motgras* and *mothok*, soon learn that in southern dialects of Dutch a *mot* is a slovenly female, and then I decide to go and visit *lijk* after all. It is indeed the dead body of a human being, but as a second meaning, it is a rope that is sewn into the edge of the sail for reinforcement, and it has an English relative in the word "leech". As an example of its use, an expression is then given, and I would give a great deal never to hear anyone use it: *hij is geheel uit de lijken geslagen*, I have no idea what kind of sentence an innocent translator might use to convey this sinister message, which might appear to involve corpses and beatings, but is in fact about being in a tizzy. Whatever the case, a *kardeel* is "a skein of several yarns twisted together". The last genuinely Dutch word to appear before *zygote*, *zymase* and *zymose*, is *zwoerd* or *zwoord*, pork crackling, pork scratchings (*heb je zwoord achter je oren?* Do you have pork scratchings behind your ears? Or: Are you deaf?) – and because every dictionary has a very last word, I find, after *zwoord*, the word *zwoordrol*, a roll of *zwoord* with a thin layer of bacon on it, peppered and salted, cooked and put in vinegar: food from a fatherland I have never known, Potgieter, Rhijnvis Feith, De Génestet, poets disappeared in time, stored with their words from the past behind a wall of McDonald's.

24

Autumn, storms, and new lessons. Strange green bunches are hanging from the *bella sombra* this year, which I have not seen in previous years, perhaps because September was an exceptionally hot month. They are too early, I did not ask for them. On the internet a beautiful young black woman shows the giant with elephant's feet that my *bella sombra* has become as a bush, as a child, but already with those inedible bunches. Inedible in two senses, she says, not tasty and also deadly, because it is poisonous, like the leaves of the oleander. Do not touch. But it is the feet that are on my mind, horizontal tree trunks, aboveground roots of enormous dimensions. There are two of them beside the fish market in the town, and you can sit on their roots, as if on a bench. I know the tree from Argentina and Brazil, where it is called *ombú*, *Phytolacca dioica*. One day it will lift up the wall, carry the garden into the air, and me with it. Xec points out a root of the palm tree and asks me if I know what it is. So now I know: not a palm root. It is in fact one of the many roots of the *bella sombra*, which has extended underground and spread beneath the palm tree, only to resurface as a strange piece of wood for people to stumble over. Through that piece of wood, all those bunches are now fed, until they fall with the rains. They have an unpleasant sweet scent of rotting, they act as if they are fruits, which they are and are not. The birds just leave them hanging there. They are disguised as fruits, they are imposters, they smell like decaying tropics, and I am the servant who must harvest them. Hundreds and hundreds lie on the wet ground, you cannot cook them, you cannot eat them. I rake them up as if they are fruit. A moral lesson, but I do not know what it is. I only obey. Laws apply here, and everyone knows them. It becomes darker earlier, the oleander that was silent all summer has new flowers but is saying nothing about his plans for the future. The Canary red admiral, too, has arrived on time, like last year and the year before he is sitting on the aeonium, shamelessly magnificent. Towards evening, he looks as if he has flown through three paint boxes at once, white insignia on the black of his or her wings, the deep red of an unknown religion, herald of the end of summer. He leaves the flowers untouched, that is for the lesser gods, the lower ranks, moth-like creatures with hummingbird wings that buzz in and out of the bougainvillea, taking a sip as they hang motionless in the air with their transparent vibrating wings, and then carrying their pleasure to somewhere I cannot follow. For the past few days, I had left them all alone after almost four months together – Madrid, Barcelona, readings, people, aeroplanes, exiled to the world. Turbulence, crowds, noise, but also the

Aeonium

major El Greco exhibition. Now I am back in the silence, but no-one shows any sign of having noticed. The black bird with his yellow bill lugs around the last of the figs that have fallen from the tree, already half rotten, and does not worry about what he will eat after that, snails crawl up the walls of the house, and when I see a lot of ants I know that something somewhere has died, all manner of things are dying now, and the ants are the clean-up service. The cactuses, who always act as if they do not need any rain, are gleaming as if they have something to say. Yesterday evening I walked along the Horse Path through a cave in the *barranco* to the beach of Canutells, where at around eight the ducks come onto the beach, as if saltwater is also their domain, lots of white ones and the occasional black one who live among the tall reeds by the small river, which is flowing again because of the rains. In the *barranco*, I suddenly saw a marten. I do not know who was more startled, me because I thought the dark rock face was suddenly moving, or him because no humans come by at that hour. He had a small, pointed, masked face, almost the colour of night. It was clear that he thought I did not belong there, a learned marten disturbed when reading a book about humans. I walked on towards the sea, a big crescent moon had risen. When I take the ship to Barcelona in three days' time, my summer will be over.

25

Intermezzo. More than two months have passed, journey to the north, Germany, Sweden, the Netherlands, into the autumn. Then back here on the island, having flown, arrived in the darkness, the garden a black hole. In the sky, white clouds, a silent squadron flying along with me up there, very light, as if it were not made of matter and knows the way to my house. The heating is not working, the house is white and cold. The loyalty of objects! Table, chairs, books, stones, shells, reading light, the little statue of Jesus as a postman with a shoulder bag and a cap, which I bought years ago in the east of Portugal. Motionless, they stand and lie there in perfect silence. A minuscule gecko like a drawing on the wall. Carrying a torch, I go into the garden to my studio. The damp has caused moss to grow on the stones of the path, by the light of the torch I see a toadstool here and there. The leaves of the aeoniums are larger than in the summer, and wider spread. On the ends of their shoots, tall, yellow flowers stand upright like inverted bunches of grapes. Beneath the palms and other trees: bedraggled leaves, branches blown off by the wind, chaos. By the studio, the cactuses stand like guards, they want nothing to do with any of this. The next day, I hear that a huge storm passed over the island a few days ago, *tramontana*, *temporal*. Hamish tells me about eight-metre waves, ships that had to stay outside the harbour. Later, Xec and Mohammed arrive, the green tips of the *pinos* that we were so worried about this summer are now lying all over the ground again. Xec breaks off a branch, pulls it apart, peers into it, removes from it something small that I cannot see, places that on a stone, kneels and takes a photograph with his mobile. Now I can see it too, enlarged. It gleams and has legs and eyes, a creature from the world of danger. So that is what my trees' enemy looks like. In another garden Xec looks after, two trees have died, split in two, fallen like men on a battlefield. The following days, rain, dirty-grey clouds. At the harbour, everything is closed, the dead season. Terraces without chairs. Where are all those waiters now? What are they doing? Are they on the island, or have they returned to the mainland, vanishing into the statistics of winter unemployment? On the quay, a lonely two-master, the *Sir Robert Baden Powell*, but no-one in sight. In my studio, behind the poetry collections, a gecko who must have been locked in upon my departure, frozen in his hibernation. On my laptop, ants appear out of nowhere, attracted by the warmth of the machine as I write. They draw meandering shapes on the screen as if they want to read what is written there. Before I left in October, I had placed the books in piles, and now I see the angry face of Canetti lying on top of something, think about what he said about Joyce as a language Dadaist and how I unexpectedly saw that refuted this evening by Adorno, as if the two books had struck up a conversation during my absence. The Adorno book has faded over the years that it spent here in a box, it is a paperback from Suhrkamp's famous rainbow series, the red is less bright, its cheap paper not so much yellowing as slightly browning, but its words still valid. It is a collection of various essays about Proust, Valéry and the Beckett of *Waiting for Godot*, and it is called *Versuch das Endspiel zu verstehen*, "Trying to Understand *Endgame*", a rather humble title.

Adorno, too, talks about Joyce. And again: for readers there is no coincidence. He cannot have read Canetti's words, but he contradicts him in a piece about Hans G. Helms, a German avant-gardist from the 1950s. I once bought a curious book by Helms: *Fa:m' Ahniesgwow*. There was an LP accompanying the book, which is at home in Amsterdam. I have not listened to that record in more than fifty years, but I remember a confused forest of voices, words linking into one another without immediate intelligibility, voices over and through one another, the school of *Finnegans Wake*. It is, says Adorno, an experiment, but one that should not be misinterpreted, "the defamatory word 'experiment' should be used positively; it is only through experimentation, not through security, that art has any chance at all," he wrote in 1960. Adorno is not a simple writer and thinker – inside his German it is sometimes as dark as it is now in my garden. He, who also considered himself a composer, writes here about music in connection with Helms, and says that the serial composers have not allowed themselves to be tempted to liquidate the *Sinn*, and that is in this case the meaning or the intelligibility, which is, at least in the Netherlands, where recently one half of the underworld has been busy liquidating the other half, a clear image. Stockhausen, too, writes Adorno, considers coherence as a *Grenzwert*, and I assume that he means: this far and no further. And when it comes to the Dadaists, a few paragraphs later he writes: "the conflict between expression and meaning in language should not simply be decided in favour of expression, as with the Dadaists." And now for the question of whether Canetti is right to call Joyce a language Dadaist. No, says Adorno (not to Canetti, but to me) in a complicated argument that begins with Proust and via involuntary memory and its Freudian associations ends up at Joyce, who uses those very associations to make the tension between expression and meaning bear fruit, since an association often attaches itself to isolated words, but derives its value from the expression of the subconscious. Adorno does believe, though, that Joyce spins out the associations so far that they sometimes detach themselves from intelligibility ("bis sie vom diskursiven Sinn sich emanzipieren"), with the added warning that Hegel's thought that the particular is the universal can become a risk when literature takes it too literally.

Meanwhile, it has become night. Barbara Sukowa sings Schönberg's *Pierrot Lunaire* in the stillness of the night. The piece dates from 1912, the recording with the Schönberg Ensemble from 1988, her voice caresses and soars and cuts with high arcs and extended notes, she sings with and then against the instruments, accentuating the all-encompassing silence outside until a distant dog barks, wanting to be part of the composition, a successful undertaking.

?26?

The set of double question marks mean that 26, within this framework, cannot be a real number, but only a question: and what do you think about all this yourself? I remember an essay? article? by Mary McCarthy about Joyce. Great admiration, but also a thought about *Finnegans Wake* as the conclusion of something, a dead end. Because what could you go on to do after *Finnegans Wake*? The most recent developments have given three possible answers to this question: back to the wear and tear of tradition, a search for a new rhetoric within the realm of images, or an adventure as far away as possible from the words, which then remain behind like cobwebs. So is that it, then? The end of the novel? No. There is still an undiscovered realm of possible variants. And perhaps the metamorphosis of reality, captured in a metamorphosis of the way of dealing with that change. But what is most likely is in fact what you see around you all the time, the apotheosis of the *manufactured* novel, fiction as a product, respectable enough to fill the increasingly slim literary supplements, which also turns them into an extension of an industry.

27

Events. Beside the studio, a fungus is growing, like an edible mushroom. He is alone, nothing around him resembles him. I see him grow a little larger every day. At the sea, grey, short waves, now and then a higher one. A small bird sits on the concrete pier, waiting for a wave to wash over. Then he pecks something up off the wet concrete that is so small it remains invisible to me even though I am standing fairly close. At home on the white wall, for days now, the triangular form of a moth, motionless.

Nearby, a gecko smaller than my little finger, a miniature. I can tell he is alive only when his position has changed, I never see him move, but every day he is somewhere else. What does he live on? Has our return disturbed his hibernation? This morning the moth was gone. But the gecko is too small to have had anything to do with that. Otherwise, not much happens. At about one o'clock, a brown cat came by, saw a black cat sitting on the wall and walked on.

28

Slowly I penetrate the secret life of cactuses. A German book with photographs and drawings shows how I can cut off a piece, and how I can plant the piece that I have cut off, but I cannot bring myself to do so. The knife looks sharp and barbaric, the greenish flesh gleams on the metal, when I look at it, I feel as if I have cut my own hand. Xec has shown me how much the column cactus has grown, at least a hand's breadth. I know the names of some of them now, even though you can never be certain. The column cactus stands next to a black aeonium. They do not know their own names, but that does not seem to bother them. I would like to be able to describe them. A rosette, a circle of glossy leaves in layers on top of one another, symmetrical. Something like an open artichoke. Mine is called Arnold Schwarzkopf, an odd name for a plant, even though his leaves are a shiny black. With a *Sempervivum* the leaves are thicker, and they stand upright, which makes them look compact. According to the book, they have as second names Killer, Gabrielle, ipf or fuego, but I do not think they answer to those names. There are hundreds of varieties, the only one in my garden that I recognise is the *Sempervivum marmoreum*, and I am not certain even of that. Subspecies *erythraeum*, it says, but that is not the sort of thing

Aeonium arboreum, *Arnold Schwarzkopf*

you say to a plant. What is astonishing is their unrelenting symmetry, a Euclidean genius has designed them, if a leaf were out of place the world would perish. This is a perfection into which I shall pry no longer, a hushed monastic order. If you look at them for long enough, you cannot help but fall silent. They do not say anything either. Last year, I read a piece by a Flemish reviewer. Apparently I pondered too much. That could be right. And I did not pay enough attention to the world. That happens when you get to my age. I think the writer was young. I did not meet him in Budapest in 1956, or in Bolivia in 1968, or in Tehran in 1976, or in Berlin in 1989, and I wonder if he ever looks at cactuses. For any length of time, I mean. In Berlin, I saw the collapse of the system that Budapest had devised forty years earlier. In Bolivia, orthodox communists told me that Che Guevara spoke no Quechua and that his struggle would fail for that reason. In 1958, in a newspaper at the airport in Cuba, I saw a young man with a beard, and yesterday, more than fifty years later, I saw that young man's brother reading out a message to the President of America. What might a Flemish critic mean when he speaks about the "world"? Which world? The world I have been watching for sixty years or the one he reads about or maybe writes about in *Dietsche Warande* or *De Standaard*? The standard of what, incidentally?

Vademecum. Go with me, Montaigne. The philosopher sits on the cover of the small book of this name, bald, a smile above his ruff, wearing a chain of office, cloak loosely around him, legs crossed, arms relaxed over his knees. He cannot hear the music by Morton Feldman that I am playing, will never hear it. To him and his era, those sounds would have been alien, an unimaginable disharmony, no matter how meditative and ethereal they sound here and now. And yet, my imagination wants to picture that for a moment, wants him, no matter how absurd and anachronistic it might be, to have said something about it in this vademecum. It is a small book published by Actes Sud, arranged alphabetically by concept. More or less at random, I have opened it at N, it seems that I wanted to catch the language in the act of moving away from us, words that after so many centuries need to be explained because they now mean something else and we no longer understand them, an anachronism in the direction of the past. When that occurs, there is a number after the word. "Nous autres naturalistes (1) estimons qu'il y aie grande et incomparable préférence de l'honneur de l'invention à l'honneur de l'allégation (2)." What I am doing here is quoting, but what he is saying is actually that people deserve incomparably more credit for coming up with something themselves than for quoting someone else. That is what we believe, he says, we proponents of the natural.

The island is empty in the winter. I have walked the long road to the sea on the south coast, to Cales Coves, where the necropolis lies high in the rocks. To the right of the road, a large, white farmhouse, half hidden. All the names here begin with *bini*, son of. *Biniadrix de baix*, *Biniadrix de dalt*, those are the names of the farms. Something is *dalt* or *baix*, upper or lower, old or new, *Binicalaf vell*, *Binicalaf nou*. And everything has remained where it was, I see the same names on old maps. I meet no-one, I know there is a gate ahead to stop the cars, anyone who wants to go further has to walk. Nearby, the last house, shutters closed, gate shut. Whoever lives there must be lonely. The Camí de Cavalls, the Horse Path, runs to the right and to the left, but from here either direction leads into a dark wood, and to the right there is also quite a climb over large blocks of stone. I want to go straight ahead now, to the water, to the narrow inlet. On my left, densely grown plants with a strange green gleam, in the summer those plants are brown from the dust on the road. Aloes with tall red flowers on long stems, like candles, *Aloe arborescens*, all over the verge small yellow flowers whose names I do not know, and a sign warning that you visit the necropolis at your own risk, but the narrow steep path to it is overgrown with a tangle of bushes, the rains of the big storm have made it slippery, you cannot even get there now. I look at the holes in the rocks where those ancient people buried their dead. They look like eye sockets without the eyes, black holes in the limy stone, too high to climb up there. Nothing can have changed here, the climate in the winter is sometimes merciless, they must have been a tough people, survivors who wanted to live by the water. The imagination wants to see those people climbing up the steep walls, wants to know what they lived on, how once upon a time they came to this island, but imagination gives me nothing I can recognise, no language, no sound, at most clichés from the wrong kinds of films, of people in animal skins swinging on creepers like apes. What kind of language did they speak? Did they come across the sea? No answer. A little later, I am at the bay, light sparkling on the water. Rocks and woodland, on both sides a worn path across the rocks, now barely passable. And in the middle of the water a boat like a vision, a sailor who has decided to seek a sheltered spot here in perfect silence and solitude. I see someone moving about on board, going by the movements a man, but it is too far to be certain. I do not know if he has seen me too. When I sit down on a rock, I hear what he must hear, the wind through the harsh bushes that grow on the hill above the rocks, the movement of the water from the sea, which I cannot see from here.

31

Transformation into a man in the crowd. My time on the island is over, airport, security. You have to walk through a childish maze, perform all the ritual actions, computer out of the bag, answer the eternal questions, stick your arms in the air just like everyone else, shoes off or not, belt off or not, no-one knows you as who you are and yet they knew you were coming, and then you are jammed with two hundred others into a cramped space, transportation. You are put in your place. You have no weapons with you, no lethal powder in your heel, you are not planning anything. A stranger sits beside you. The same words as always, heard them a thousand times. If cabin pressure drops, something will fall from the space above, says the voice. Hundreds of flights, but the cabin pressure has never dropped, I've never had to strap on the lifejacket, never ended up in the sea, never drowned, but for a moment the thought of death skims past, as fleeting as your sleeping neighbour's aftershave. As we are about to land, everyone grabs their mobile phone, an extension of the body. At the next airport you have to wait a few hours among the food outlets and fashion stores, electronics and bars, you sit and watch others going past with their rolling suitcases, a long procession that never stops, then it all happens again, you take your seat once again, strap yourself in for the second time, you are launched upwards into that other element, you see the tops of the clouds, where human beings do not belong because they cannot walk there, sometimes a scrap of land becomes visible, red-brown soil, a river, forests, a lonely house, like the house you came from, where someone is sitting and looking at the trees, who stands up, goes inside to fetch the rake, does not hear or see the aeroplane above, but with long, sweeping movements rakes up the leaves that fell last night.

32

Another country, winter, cold, a big house full of books, alone in the woods. A ridge, large farms, slanting roofs under the snow, northern Cubism. Silence. I hear my laptop humming, a drawn-out mechanical and monotonous sound that is waiting for words and has nothing to do with the sea or the wind in the trees. I look at the letters of the alphabet, the punctuation marks, at arrows and secret messages I still do not understand, I am six years old, I put letters together until they become words, I have done so all my life. I have cast off my identity as man in the crowd, or so it seems, I see a great tit in the hedge, a deer silhouetted against the snow, two people cross-country skiing and leaving a trail. For years now, I have come here for the first months of the year. On the last day of the vanishing year, we gather with a few friends, stand on the balcony at twelve o'clock and look at the lights on the horizon, where the fireworks are going off. It is quiet here, a few bangs, nothing more. I know the names of the farms I cannot see right now, Krottental, Pfaffenweiler, Albishaus, as soon as the snow is gone I will be able to walk there. A labyrinthine network of narrow roads through meadows and high forests connects those large and silent houses to one another, usually there is no-one to be seen, sometimes someone walks across a yard or a dog barks. The cows stand in long rows in the big sheds, as you go past they look at you with the incomparable gaze that Gombrowicz wrote a passage about in his Argentinian diary, which essentially said that he had looked into the abyss of existence. On bright days I see the mountains, sharp and shining in the distance. Fields that slowly descend to a phalanx of woodland that looks black now, and then more fields beyond, a ridge of hills. To the left, seen from the window, a narrow country road, even before it gets light I hear the snowplough going past, the radio warns of slippery roads, everything is the German antithesis of my Spanish summers. Groceries a few kilometres away, a peaceful little town with a medieval feel, a dark and squat inn with no television, where you pull up a chair at large tables for a plate of *Kesselfleisch* or *Flädlesuppe*, among the others with their dialect, hard to understand at times, in which *mir* is not the dative form of the first-person singular pronoun, but the first-person plural: *mir kommet, wir kommen*, we come. Outside, painted houses, coats of arms and years in Gothic script, along the roads and paths chapels to Mary and crucifixes, with Christ in his loincloth hanging cold and forlorn in the snow. Somewhere in the countryside, a *Kneipe* called Kongo, where silent men sit with half-litre glasses of Hefeweizen that they take an eternity to drink. Sometimes someone says something, and then there is a brief conversation, which falls silent after a few minutes as if everything that has been said now needs to be contemplated. The outsider who is me reads the *Schwäbische Zeitung*, news from the world and news from the region. You eat *Bretkned-lesuppe* or *Sauerkäse mit Trauerrand*, a pickled cheese with onions, surrounded by thin slices of blood sausage, black with speckles of white, cheese in mourning. I once asked why the pub is called Kongo. The answer goes back to the time of Lumumba. Things take a long time to change around here.

In the days of the Congolese civil war, when Patrice Lumumba was executed, this pub had the first television in the area. The place was just called Grüner Baum back then. Farmers came from all over the area to watch black people killing each other, the toxic legacy of Leopold II, the world of Joseph Conrad, still valid today. When the weather is good, you can sit outside and look into the valley and listen to the slow conversations around you, which you do not understand. The world of Berlin or of the Landeshauptstadt Stuttgart seems infinitely far away. In the hour when I wrote these pages nothing and no-one came by on the country road outside, not a car, not a person and not a deer. If I were to stand up and walk beyond the bend in the road, I would see the hawk that always sits there on a high branch, looking out over the landscape as I do, and this week I saw a dead fox nailed to a stable door, as if crucified. In the evening, when the silence outside is solid, the world presents itself on the screen, bombings, war, murders. Ukraine, Paris, Nigeria, Isis, Boko Haram, Charlie Hebdo, everything is painted on the glass, as if you are looking through a tunnel into the distance and the landscapes outside and the books inside no longer exist. Demonstrations in Dresden, where no Muslims live, but even so the people marching there are still scared of Muslims. I see European heads of state demonstrating arm in arm in Paris for freedom of expression, and then I see them again a few weeks later in Riyadh, at the funeral of the desert king of that land, where a man has just been condemned to one thousand lashes for his opinions. I read a history of Venice, the bestial murders and rapes in the Constantinople of 1453, Christians against Muslims and then the other way around, yesterday's newspaper, the constants of history. And with the news from

Greece, I see the Acropolis in the background and feel like an ancient Japanese man who has retreated from the world and hears the sounds of a distant battle. Until what age do you need to concern yourself with the world? I was born before a war, my father died in that war, after that there were wars for as long as I have lived. Once, when that war had turned cold, I had to fear mass destruction, everywhere I have travelled in the world, history has shown her face in constant repetition but not yet as a farce. Revolutions, battles of liberation, colonial wars, oppression, guerrilla warfare, terrorism and counterterrorism, there is something humbling about being a contemporary of violence and acting as if you know what you might be able to do about it, even if only because you are already on a particular side, a member of the West, a citizen of Europe, everything that Danton realised too late, halfway through the terror. It seems you have decided that soldiers are going to Mali, where you once travelled in other times, just as you walked around the Bolivia of Che Guevara, the Hungary of October '56, the sealed-off Germany of the DDR and the Spain of Franco and the violent ETA. You were against the war in Iraq and you wrote about that but the catastrophe was infinitely greater than you had expected. Napoleon did not want to heed Talleyrand and went to Moscow anyway, Hitler got stuck in Stalingrad and Bush and Blair had no Talleyrand at all. It is not as if you have not seen the world or listened to conflicting opinions, perhaps you have sometimes chosen sides, but you do not remember if that helped, maybe you have never understood the essential mechanisms of disaster and it is time for you to disappear into your garden while the rest irrevocably rush on in the world as a misunderstanding according to laws that, whether you read Thucydides or Ranke, Gibbon or Tony Judt, never seem to change. History is made of people, the dead are the material and with the dead come numbers. Once, as a child, you saw a dead English pilot hanging from his parachute, before that you saw the bodies of German soldiers being recovered from the water, long grey coats dripping. You have forgotten none of this, so perhaps you understand the photographs of the forced recruits from Ukraine as future victims in a different way than others do, knowing that in the next photograph they will not be standing but lying down. You have looked into the faces of soldiers since you were six years old, German faces, Iranian faces, Spanish and Colombian helmets, you are plastered all over inside with newspapers full of deaths right up until today, even if you yourself are safe, you are smeared with the filth of war that will accompany your days until their end, whether you want it or not. This week, Auschwitz was commemorated here, last year in Krakow you saw discount taxis and tour buses to the camp as a form of the bitterest irony, you saw survivors and what the history of violence had written in their faces, and your gaze will be contaminated until you disappear.

33

Sometimes it happens, suddenly, unexpectedly. You hear a sound behind all the noise, you stand still and listen. Among the excess of the world, you find in music a sanctuary where, albeit briefly, you can pause, take a breath.

Cello with voices, instruments. Short movements, ecstatic sound, elongated, then a fanning pattern of other, deeper voices, the cello with abrupt notes that want to go up, silence, the same cello, deep, then the distant voices again, there is an enormous church of air around this music, the choir is infinitely far away and speaks with the cello, I do not need to know what they are singing, everything is in keeping with the landscape outside, something is going on in which words have no place, the high, gurgling sound of an instrument I do not know, music that does not wish to be named, a sanctuary of sound to which I am barely admitted, if at all, radiance, a message from beyond time that was written down by someone. It keeps wanting to spirit me away, it is ethereal and untouchable and defies description. Sofia Gubaidulina, *The Canticle of the Sun*, played by Pieter Wispelwey.

34

Not only do Hungarians have a language that seems to belong with nothing else, that language also has a rhythm and a melody that are capable of changing and overpowering any other language that a Hungarian speaks. It reminds me of a machine gun that makes a noise without firing any deadly shots, rat-a-tat-a-tat, and I catch myself in an unknown form of enjoyment when I listen to a completely incomprehensible conversation between Hungarian friends. With most languages you hear, there is some point of anchor or place of refuge, but not here, and that in turn takes you to the secret of language itself, mouths producing sounds, throat, uvula, palate, lips combining to form a set of instruments with which thoughts and emotions are expressed, completely obvious to the speakers but shutting me out. In ascending order of alienation, I have recently read three Hungarian writers, Miklós Bánffy in Dutch and English, Péter Esterházy in German and Miklós Szentkuthy in French and English. Bánffy is the most accessible, his trilogy is a classic panorama of glory and decline, in which the alienation comes more from ignorance of the finer points and the unimaginable complications of the parliamentary history of the Habsburg monarchy than because of the classic love story that runs through the three volumes like a sort of *Gone with the Wind*. As a member of parliament, the novel's protagonist, Count Bálint Abády, has a good instinct for the nightmarish frivolity with which the various parties are heading for catastrophe and has to watch helplessly in the parliamentary theatre as the clock of fate keeps on ticking until the bomb literally explodes in Serbia, the Austria and Hungary of the k. und k. are torn asunder, the Danube monarchy degenerating into a splintered map of languages and nationalities. Hungary loses large territories in the process, which will lead to major problems in the years to come because of the Hungarian-speaking minorities in all its neighbouring countries, and this will be continued after the Second World War when Transylvania falls to Romania. Count Miklós

Bánffy, who bears a strong resemblance to his own protagonist, came from one of the oldest and most distinguished
families in Transylvania, then still part of Hungary, later of
Communist Romania. He owned extensive lands, which he
would lose twice, palace and all, the first time briefly to
Béla Kun and his Republic of Councils, the second time to
Communist Romania. He was, for that time, before the First
World War, a liberal and progressive member of parliament
and later even the Minister for Foreign Affairs. He wrote his
memoirs about those days in 1932, published in English by
Arcadia Books with the title *The Phoenix Land*, on reflection
a rather sad title because the Hungarian phoenix, after its
first resurgence in 1921, was shot down again in the aftermath
of the Second World War, and this time for good. There is also
an amusing side to those memoirs, because Bánffy, during Béla
Kun's short-lived reign of terror, lost all his possessions and
lived as an impoverished exile in the Netherlands, where he
kept his head above water as a portrait painter until the next
revolution when, as Minister for Foreign Affairs, he attempted
to avert the imminent consequences of the treaty of Trianon,
in which Hungary would be plucked like a chicken. He writes
with a lot of humour about that brief period as an impoverished portrait painter of wealthy ladies in The Hague. I
first heard about him from a friend who has worked all over
the world as a diplomat, Teheran, Kosovo, Jakarta, and who,
when she discovered that I still had not read the book she had
so highly recommended, sent me the three parts of the Transylvanian Trilogy in English. She is a great lover of Russian
literature and, above all, Pushkin, and later I understood what

appealed to her so much about Bánffy, and why she had thought it would interest me. She was not wrong. I, too, still have a taste for what literature surrendered first to modernism and later to the world of the image. In the 1930s, people could still write that way. Half a lifetime after that publication, Péter Esterházy, a Hungarian author far more modern in essence, praised Bánffy's irony and intelligence because of the sweeping portrait of an era that he painted, capturing a lost class that Esterházy himself would portray so differently. Patrick Leigh Fermor, who sixty years later would write a foreword for the English edition of the Transylvanian Trilogy, had become acquainted with that world during his iconic journey on foot through Europe in the period between the wars – I recall photographs of uniformed Hungarian counts and barons in which they look like extinct species of birds – but other Hungarian friends I asked did not seem to know Bánffy's book. The original edition, which in Hungarian is called *Megszámláltattál*, was published in 1934, and in the Communist era the class enemy's book was forbidden. Bánffy's estate was expropriated, his palace destroyed, he himself had remained alone in Romania, and it was not until much later that he returned to Budapest to die. I do not know whether Esterházy's praise has to do with the fact that he, too, is from an ancient and even more powerful family, I never asked him. In the Netherlands, only the first two volumes of Bánffy have been published, by Atlas Contact. In the Dutch translation, the first part is called *Geteld, geteld*, and in English *They Were Counted*, a title connected to the Bible's cautionary *mene, mene, tekel, upharsin*, the writing on the wall that calls down all the misfortune that is to come. The English edition I read compares the book to Lampedusa's *Il Gattopardo*. There, too, a grand romantic story is set in a feudal world that is doomed to disappear. Bánffy's trilogy is a love story of the kind we know from the nineteenth century, an idealistic protagonist of the sort we have encountered in Chekhov's *The Cherry Orchard* and *Three Sisters*, with here as a counterweight a cousin tragically heading for an alcoholic downfall and squandering and forfeiting his estate at the gaming table. For the modern reader, this summons up a fascinating and melancholy image of a company revolving around itself, with intrigues and gossip, costumed balls and hunts, a book like a film, splendour pregnant with its own inevitable decline. Miklós Bánffy, who as the director of the Hungarian State Theatres gave Béla Bartók's work a chance in Budapest, managed his estate in Transylvania and as Minister for Foreign Affairs negotiated Hungary's entry to the League of Nations and also wrote a book in which the tragic history of his country is etched in an unforgettable way, has remained hidden from the rest of Europe for too long. Yalta drew a dividing line across this continent, a wound that can be healed only slowly. I remember seeing the three volumes once in a bookshop somewhere in South America, leafing through and, intimidated by their bulk, leaving them there. I was wrong to have done so.

Not only the trilogy, but also his own history ended tragically. During the Second World War, he had pleaded with the dictator, Admiral Horthy, for Hungary to break free from its alliance with Germany, and so the Nazis, during their retreat, destroyed his beloved palace in Cluj, in what is now

Romania. By a strange twist of fate, the Transylvanian nobility, unlike the Hungarians, had their property returned, as far as was possible. Jaap Scholten has written a fine book about this vanished human species with the meaningful title of *Kameraad Baron* (Comrade Baron), in which he depicts the sometimes tragic and humiliating fate of the *ci-devants* after the war, the dark flip side of the former splendour most of them did not even know, nobility as condemnation, imprisonment, torture, poverty, survival as a maid or lorry driver, who in most cases could do nothing with their penniless estates and dilapidated castles.

Esterházy's father was also a count, and the book his son wrote deals in part with that same confusing Hungarian history, and because Esterházy named every single one of his ancestors after his father, from the Middle Ages to the current day, the first volume of his book *Harmonia Cælestis* (in English, *Celestial Harmonies*)[3] has become a historical aria of insanity in which his father founds schools, builds churches, is a minister in one century and is hanged and shot dead in another. A man who has many ancestors and access to their written history has many fathers, all of whom he can call my father or sometimes *myfather*, just as he calls himself, in the third person, my father's son. I do not know whether this is true, but I feel that this book could not have been written anywhere other than in Hungary, as if there is some quirk in the Hungarian spirit, a tightrope-walking absurdism that does not exist elsewhere. Maybe, I think presumptuously, it has to

3 Translated into English by Judith Sollosy.

do with the continent's lines of longitude, as you move to the east you find the Kafkas and the Bulgakovs, the Čapeks, the Esterházys and the Szentkuthys. In order to find out what kind of world this book is set in, you need only click once on the Esterházy family online, human cockerels in uniforms decorated with insignia, counts, princes, bishops, generals, ministers, bellies and bouffants, thoroughbred horses with the accompanying wives and palaces, and their late descendant who, after the disappearance of Communism, wanted nothing of all that property returned, has written an anachronistic masterpiece in which he describes and simultaneously ridicules the past in such a way that the tragic and the comic enter into an irresistible chemical affinity. In that world, a listening device can be inside a confessional from Metternich's time, a son can describe his parents' first fellatio with anthropological and hilarious accuracy, one of his fathers gives ten gold ducats to the executioner before he is beheaded and a twentieth-century author can fill endless pages with an extremely detailed list of family jewels that could fill a museum, and the visual manner of writing ensures that, in addition to everything else, this book is also an illustrated *Zeitgeschichte*. This writer, who studied mathematics and once worked at a Hungarian ministry as a systems analyst, has described the system from which he comes, which was to clash so flagrantly with the system that would destroy that earlier world, as a Grand Guignol of human possibilities, from heroism to betrayal. With the fragmentation bomb of his writing, he blows his family's past into thousands of shards, while holding it together with the notion of a family as a historical unit, a miracle. It is not harmonious and it certainly is not heavenly. The second volume of the book is set in the twentieth century. As with Bánffy, under the dictatorship of Béla Kun, the Hungarian part of the family loses money, palaces and estates, and later everything and for ever. The decline has its own hilarity, from the very first sentence: "Your Excellency, my lady, if I might put it this way, by your leave, the communists are here." But the tragedy of Péter Esterházy was that he did not know the second volume would be followed by a third, a volume that in German was given the title *Verbesserte Ausgabe*, or improved edition, but better was bitter, because after *Harmonia Cælestis* became a bestseller in Hungary, Esterházy, who had intended his book about all those fathers as a tribute to his own actual father and the way he had endured the loss of his position and possessions, along with the accompanying humiliations caused by the new Communist elite's resentment and pettiness, discovered that his father was not the hero he had thought but, on the contrary, had worked as an agent for the Hungarian Stasi, had written reports of conversations with people from his own class, and had, in short, committed treason. Treason against a past, a family, perhaps too against the book that the son had written about that family's past. What is expressed in that third, unforeseen volume is shock, a sense of deep and tragic disappointment. The father is already dead by that point, there can be no discussion, nothing will be resolved. He has worked on his book for ten years, the first reviews are coming out, and now it is as if this great work is being undermined by this scandal. And yet the writer does not desert his father but finds a tone that does justice both to the tragedy and to the absurdity of what happened. That tone has to do with humour and intelligence, but also with the style and the history of a family, which Esterházy describes in the first two volumes with affection and irony, and so the drama of his father, however painful, seems to fit into the family history after all, as it is both family and history.

As far as the fortunes of their families are concerned, the Esterházys and the Bánffys have a few things in common, a past that has irrevocably disappeared, the world of the *ci-devants*. The Esterházys belonged to the Hungarian and Austrian nobility, the Bánffys came from Transylvania, which was once a part of Hungary but after the war fell to the Romania of Ceausescu and the Securitate, the world of Comrade Baron. Esterházy is without a doubt the greater writer, he had the benefit of the later birth. But to understand the fate of that part of Europe, both books are indispensable. You could also say that Esterházy's later book gives a better understanding of Bánffy's classic novel, as if the splendour and the vibrancy of the depiction in *Harmonia Cælestis* places Bánffy's lost and silent world in a new light that allows you to see everything better.

35

After a few days on the trapeze, I am ready for the landscape in front of me. Breathtakingly white, marked only by the tracks of foxes, deer and cats. I understand that the foxes and the deer have to pass through the deep snow when they want to get from here to there, but why the cats? Norbert and Claudia, the people who look after this house and the woods, live across the narrow country road. Norbert works at a *Käserei*, keeps an eye on the extensive woodland and feeds the deer when it gets too cold. The day before yesterday it was minus 13 at night. He has a hunting diploma, but he is not too fond of shooting, does so only when he has to. Norbert and Claudia have four children, two of whom have left home. We also see the grandchildren at birthday parties, a great joy. They speak the local dialect, and when they do this quickly, and to one another, I lose great chunks of the conversation, but they file off the sharpest edges for us and throw in the music for free. Its tonality is not easy to describe, it is attractive but I would not be able to say precisely why, let alone imitate it. Speaking languages has to do with musicality and imitation more than with intelligence, but when you attempt to imitate a dialect among the people who speak it you fall into a sociological trap, you are infringing upon ownership. Anyone who attempts to do that might be better off heading straight to the circus or an asylum, language is, after all, acquired property, you can't just take it away.

The question remains: why the cats? There are four of them plus one. One is ginger and is permitted to enter the house across the way, a privilege. She is friends with Trixy, a black-and-white Chinese-looking dog two decimetres tall, who, as far as I am concerned, is one of those beloved creatures who make life on Earth easier to bear, if only because she sometimes looks as if she has read everything by Li Po. The other four cat-creatures are diehards, they live outside and in the shed inside a big cardboard box of hay, room for four. They seem to like us well enough, but they never come too close. Two grey ones, two white and brown. They are the philosophers, they venture outside and sit alone far away in the meadow and think stubbornly, even now, when there is a lot of snow. Sometimes they roll in it, and I wonder what that feels like. When the layer of snow is high, as it is now, they have to put one foot at a time in the thick white mass, a strange way to move forward. When there is less snow, their tracks are easy to recognise, and when there is more, the holes become wider and deeper. Fox and deer leave different marks, the cats' tracks can be seen by satellite, like holes that have been scooped out with a ladle, maybe because they are in less of a hurry than the wild animals, who always have a hunter in the back of their minds. It is past five now, it has been foggy all day, a white shroud that lifted a little only two hours ago, so that above the black forest in the distance streaks of orange slowly turn grey. While there was fog outside, I read, which is what I meant about the trapeze. I feel as if I have spent hours on a trapeze, some books do that to you. No safety net, the risk of the *salto mortale*, that happens with books, too.

Pirouettes, strange lurches, headstands, the occasional cropper, that is what you get when you read Miklós Szentkuthy, the third of the three Hungarians. Show us, think the readers, but that is the problem – where to begin? Only some of his books have been translated into English, and you are basically threatened with a death sentence if you copy too much from them. (Quoting is copying.) Then why not put it into your own words? You should be able to do that, shouldn't you? English, the world language into which the least is translated, a combination of arrogance and provincialism: knowing for certain that everyone reads you anyway, and believing that enough has already been written in your own language. Only two per cent and a crumb of the entire world's literature is published in America, such a meagre harvest that you realise why Americans sometimes understand so little about the world – and that means Japan, Chile, Norway or Hungary, but it does at least include books by Szentkuthy, who has been dead for more than thirty years.

36

An example of being on the trapeze: cactuses and a sonata by Haydn. What? This is what I mean: Szentkuthy's book *Towards the One & Only Metaphor* consists of 112 small chapters, and at the front of the book are short lines describing the contents of each of those chapters. Chapter 22: "My essence: an absolute and unbroken need for intensity. But let there also be orgasm: form!" That was the first swing on the trapeze. Chapter 98: "What if a person is not truly born for anything?" Chapter 86: "A departed person. Lack, absence: absurd mathematical points of departure and everyday realities." No, perhaps that is not something for Kansas, and maybe not for the Netherlands either, given my dizziness.

And yet, take my last swing on the trapeze, chapter 43: "A Haydn sonata and a cactus. My experiments at a novel: they are that in a concrete *biological* sense." And finally chapter 70: "My style is a rag like St. Francis' clothes; my style is tuberculosis like St. Theresa's; my style is blood like that of the martyrs." Here, mine and his constantly run together. By Teresa, I think he means the one from Ávila, the one from Lisieux has little business being here, but with him you never know. After all these spiritual exercises, and I do not mean that cynically or satirically, I felt the need to look at those tracks in the snow for a while. Szentkuthy occupies my mind, but these are exercises that do not leave a person untouched. How can they, written as they are by someone with universal pretensions? A man who can do much and wants to do it all. In the books I have read in translation alone, the diversity of subjects is as overwhelming as the extent of his huge library, mathematics at a high level, biology as fascination, classical philology and a hundred side paths, these are the preoccupations of someone who has both written about the importance of candlelight and chandeliers in the life of Casanova and penned a fictionalised biography of Goethe. Again, chapter 43, a Haydn sonata and a cactus. I have Haydn's six late sonatas here, played by Glenn Gould at the Columbia 30th Street Studio in 1981 and released in 1992. That is the first half of Szentkuthy's proposition. The other half is that cactus, and the fourth word in the first sentence of this book was cactuses. Two years ago, prompted by a book by Karel Čapek published in 1929, I planted a number of cactuses in my

Spanish garden, so this section seems to have been written for me. (There is only one way of reading, and that is via delusions of reference – everything was written solely for the person who has the book in their hand at that moment.) As I write on, Gould, in 1981, plays sonata number 42 as an illustration of Szentkuthy's proposition: the difference between that sonata and my cactus is the difference between the classical-rational structure of a "work" on the one hand, and biological forms (my cactus – as I am writing this, I see him before me as though I were looking into my garden in Spain) on the other. "My own writings for the time being," says Miklós Szentkuthy, "belong to the cactus category: if I can have a role in literature it is the direct tangibility of biological lines and forms of instinct in my sentences. 'Experimental novel' was said about *Prae* in more than one place, by which one was supposed to understand an anachronistic relic of the old-fashioned mood of the 19th century." *Prae*, in spite of the huge reputation that the book has in Hungary, has been translated into few other languages, which prompts both suspicion and curiosity. But there is enough that has been translated, including the *Marginalia on Casanova*, in itself only the first part of his *St Orpheus Breviary*, ten volumes of which have been published in Hungary. It is a wild book, his *Casanova*, and from the introduction I understand that, strangely enough, it came about after Szentkuthy read a study by Karl Barth on Paul's Epistle to the Romans, a study based on a sentence-by-sentence analysis of that letter. According to Zéno Bianu's foreword, Szentkuthy was so impressed by that method that he decided to apply it to the autobiography of Casanova. And this is where the chandeliers and the candles come in, the balls and the masks, Venice but above all the chapters about asceticism, strictness, and about the ability to "reconcile elegance and bestiality – or, if one prefers, boudoir and theology", from which a different, more metaphysical Casanova emerges than the libidinous image that has been passed down to us. Years ago, I had the opportunity to interview Fellini about his Casanova film. If I could have read this book back then, I would have been better prepared. Fellini detested Casanova, whom he saw as an *automaton*, the mechanical and obsessive seducer of women, played by Donald Sutherland. The image Szentkuthy presents of him is far more nuanced, and this begins with the saint's life with which he precedes the book, the hagiography of St Alphonsus Maria di Liguori, a *vita* so far from what is the norm in this genre that I thought it was a colossal joke, complete with wigs full of lice and bishops' mitres that look like leather-bound wine lists, a shrieking queen of Naples who claims that the saint has written his *theologia moralis* to please the revolutionaries and then throws a red stiletto shoe at the saint. The omniscient internet relieved me of this delusion, Alphonsus really existed, and he was also really a saint, you can pray to him.

Better to contemplate the photograph of the Hungarian writer for a while. Meanwhile, Gould plays on in my room, and he does so as brilliantly as ever but with this music also a little like a music box, a frivolous way to describe a classical-rational structure, but perhaps a cactus is a better match for me. The photograph is on the cover of the French edition of another very different book by Szentkuthy, which I bought

Portrait of Miklós Szentkuthy on
La Confession frivole

years ago in Paris: *La Confession frivole*, a book that confused me back then with the amount of chatter in it, because, trapeze or no trapeze, Szentkuthy is something like a volcano in constant eruption, and you can only flee or keep watching from as close as possible. Who was the man in profile on that cover? He is looking straight ahead, but actually it seems as if he is still looking at me even though he is turned away, perhaps peeping at me out of the corner of his eye. It is a magnificent profile, the photograph must have been taken early in the previous century. A large and very fine black hat, a bow tie with polka dots, this gentleman knew how to dress. Black, curly hair peeping out from under that hat, beneath which that remarkable brain sits, a clairvoyant, speculating, essayistic, confabulating mind that constantly presents you with merciless surprises, trips you up with paradoxes, does not shy away from apparent incompatibilities: Catholicism and eroticism, rationalism and mysticism, an extremely well-read writer who translated Joyce and Swift, sized up Goethe, followed Casanova for the length of an intriguing book and, according to some people, with his *Prae*, wrote one of the masterpieces of the past century, so that he may pit himself against Proust, Rabelais, Joyce, a notion that he himself – probably correctly – described as nonsense. I remember years ago asking my friend the essayist and philosopher László Földényi to tell me something about him – what I remember is an intriguing story about a man with a library of more than twenty-five thousand books who, like a spider in his web, had spent the endless years of the dictatorship writing and reading in Rákosi's communist Budapest, forbidden to write or at least to publish, an erotomaniac who worked on an enormous series, each volume of which would begin with a provocative saint's life – in short, enough to pique the curiosity. And now? Maybe it is dangerous in a time of manufactured books to venture into the territory of a man who wanted to write a book about everything and who, in a room in Budapest, took his heroic quest to the bitter end, leaving an oceanic oeuvre to sail upon or to drown within, a work written so systematically that, in my opinion, it does not need to be read systematically, as it is a mine with entrances on every side. But no matter where you enter, you will meet the same magician, who will surprise you again and again with unexpected ways of thinking, suggestions and opinions far removed from canonical philosophy, a manner of thinking you have encountered nowhere before, one that will not let you go.

37

It has grown dark outside. Stars, Orion in his place among the other constellations, the blind hunter who rules north and south. So still, nothing is moving.

This is the day when the 27 will talk to the Greeks in Brussels, guilt and penance. Will we remain 28 or not? And in Minsk, three men and a woman are trying to avert further disaster. The whole day I have been watching great tits trying to find something left amidst the snow in the withered hedges. They tap their beaks against the wood, in search of whoever lives there. Gould has finished playing, the classical-rational structure of Haydn evaporating into the silence after the last note. Somewhere in a Spanish garden stands a cactus, a green column with six seams, who if I were to cut him open would reveal white flesh, which would grow back again. No-one made him, he just grew. He did not come up with the plan himself, he already had it within him when I planted him, complete with "biological lines and forms of instinct", as Szentkuthy sees his writing. Cactus or sonata, that is the question.

38

On an island, are you further away from the world? In spite of the media, whose reports there are the same as elsewhere, the answer is yes, but difficult to prove because it is about atmospheric factors, such as snow, winter, cold, language. It is northern here, and German. The aura is not that of the Mediterranean, my summer habitat. Since I last wrote, the two simultaneous poker games, Ukraine and Greece, Minsk and Grexit, have moved on. Result still undecided. Some people are better at lying than others, but that will not necessarily help them. I am still a child of the war, and after that the Cold War, I get most of the news here in German, only buy the foreign newspapers on a Saturday in Lindau or Bregenz. Everyone who sees through the lies writes about the people who have not seen through the lies. Pictures can lie too, but usually not as successfully. A flag on a building, a dead child, a burnt-out hospital. This inevitably makes the war in the east of Ukraine a continuation of something that happened long ago, you do not simply dismiss something like that if you have any form of memory. What did Paul Valéry say? "The memory is the future of the present." Long lines of men who have lost, that was how I saw the German columns pass by in 1944, their gait is familiar. Now I see a president pinning medals to the chests of men who look over his shoulder and into a black hole. At the back of that black hole, I am sitting with my newspaper, looking this man in the face, a face that cannot see me, that belongs with the shapes of corpses under cloths or dirty blankets that have been tossed over them, empty shells, faces you saw seventy years ago and which then were made of paper can now talk, but say nothing because the fury and the despair are too great.

And Greece? Is that closer because I recognise the landscapes, the Mediterranean way of speaking, the fragments of Thucydides and Polybius left inside my head? Or even older, as in Homer, when, in those slowly dancing lines that we had to decipher, the war could be about a woman, something I understood better at the age of fourteen? Because often I no longer remember the words but can still read the letters on the signs that are carried in processions with the Acropolis in the background? How long ago was that, those first Greek lessons, Xenophon, yet more stories of exclusion and war? And again, images that are figuratively connected to all that. German troops on Crete, partisans, executions. Patrick Leigh Fermor in a German uniform kidnapping a German general. Is Schäuble wrong because he speaks German too? Is Varoufakis wrong because he, as the newspapers here write, is biting on granite with Schäuble? Is the sun child setting the stakes too high in his game of poker against the winter men? Men without ties against men with ties – does that mean something? Can you do sums better in a tie? Today they delivered their new proposals, and the reactions will come tomorrow. Waiting for the teachers' answer, moving on or repeating a year, the headmaster in a wheelchair. It snowed again last night, as if what was written yesterday had to be deleted.

39

22.2. For the first time a date, and really only because, contrary to my intentions, politics has come up for discussion after all. When I began these notes, without thinking too much about it, I came up with the working title *Diario Novo*. That is not Spanish (*nuevo*) and not Italian (*nuovo*), maybe I was secretly hoping it would be Portuguese. I tried to explain my connection to Spain in my book *Roads to Santiago*. This has to do with the imagination of Cervantes and the severity of Zurbarán, the all or nothing of the civil war, the harsh climate of the Castilian *meseta*, with things you discover by yourself in another culture, an essential affinity that you cannot explain and that you have not chosen, because then why not the splendour of Italy or the seductive melancholy of Portugal or the clear austerity of the country where you were born, whose language is the only one in which you want to write?

It is even doubtful whether this is in fact a diary, perhaps it is more like a book of days, something to help you preserve the occasional something from the stream of what you think, what you read, what you see, certainly not a book for confessions. The theme was *il faut cultiver notre jardin* until I realised it was more a case of my garden teaching me, a long summer on an island provides the opportunity, away from the current affairs of home, withdrawing to live with books and music, with the landscapes and sea views of an island. When you have lived a long time, so much becomes unimportant, you have seen much of the world, you recognise the settings of the events on television because you have walked in those places, the balcony of Allende or Cristina Kirchner, students demonstrating in the familiar streets of Hong Kong, or the Popemobile in Seoul, a terrorist attack in Sydney, the world is becoming pushy and greedy, you would like to retreat like an old Japanese man into some monastery or other, but the world still wants all kinds of things from you, you are far from having detached yourself and others keep calling you back, partly because you wrote and said things in the past, it is not that easy to escape from yourself, the compromise you have chosen is that of the island in the summer and the winter months near the Alps, where I am now, looking at a landscape that is so white that I have to close my eyes. This morning Simone saw six deer, one leading the way, she said, they were walking in a line across the open ground, from one wood to another. They are always so very visible out there in the field, and it is usually the last one who stops, hesitates, before joining the others again. She had been afraid that the last one, who was the smallest, would take fright and go back alone. There is a new law here banning the feeding of deer in the winter. Norbert, who has a manger deep in the forest, where he always took hay in the bitter cold, is sad about that. He does not like the thought of a deer dying of starvation so close to humans. It may be about natural selection, he says, but it is not natural when we interfere in this negative way either.

40

This *diario novo* is not about committing my soul to paper or investigating my conscience, that was never the intention, if only because shame and/or calculation would undermine its authenticity. But what is it, then? In the past, I have kept a diary at irregular intervals, which I never revisit. Two years ago, however, I typed out around a hundred pages from 1980, sometimes with embarrassment at the intended honesty, sometimes with disdain for the theatrics, or boredom at the inanity, it can never be an honest undertaking. And there are, at least in my case, things that are no-one else's business. Or, as I wrote in *The Foxes Come at Night* at the end of my story "Heinz": "We are our secrets, and, if all goes well, we will take them with us to where no-one can touch them." Besides, there is a hidden pleasure in keeping secrets.

41

Objection. Then why do you read diaries? In the top corridor of this house they are grouped more or less together, Julien Green, Michel Leiris, André Gide. All in German, translated from French. I open Julien Green at a random page and find myself at 14.2.1943. "Sad to be what one is. If one is sad enough, one will, I think, change." Was the French word for *one* used here too? The Dutch equivalent, *men*, as used by

Kouwenaar, is magnificent in his poetry because it contains an almost mystical form of universality. It does not work in the same way here. Green is, I believe, talking primarily about himself. I try it in a different way: "Sad to be who you are. If you're sad enough, you'll change, I think." The volume in which this appears is called in French *L'œil de l'ouragan*. The Eye of the Hurricane. But what was the hurricane in 1943? The war? And did Green change, or was that not necessary? On the cover, words by Albert von Schirnding from the *Süddeutsche Zeitung*: "[. . .] countless figures appear, notably André Gide, who is portrayed very effectively with his character flaws." So, it's off to Gide, same year, same day, but there it is about the superiority of the Anglophones, which is said to stem from their Protestant education. Two weeks later, on March 1st, Leiris is not only in the war for real (as all three of them are in 1943), but also within a dream. He is in an atelier with a friend. In that dream, the friend suddenly lies down on the ground and tells him to do the same. The occupier has posted a notice all over Paris with the words "On the ground – or adieu", because anyone who does not follow the order will receive the death penalty. The Allied invasion has just begun (here Leiris's dream was the father of the thought, the invasion did not happen until over a year later) – time to prepare for the final, decisive fight. German patrols will search all the houses and summarily execute anyone who has not followed the order. Leiris concludes the entry for that day with "terrified, my friend and I lay on the ground". Leafing back through Green, I see that the quote above was not from 1943 but from 1945. So now I try to find a date on which Green and Gide wrote in their diaries on the same day. For added interest, Green is in America and Gide is in Tunis, but on 19 February 1943, Green writes about the war in Tunis: "The Germans have captured Nefta and Tozeur. For most people, this is just one report of many, but the memories it evokes for me! These oases are, in my opinion, an almost perfect image of happiness on Earth." He says here "me", as if lending his memory to the other me who is writing these sentences so many years later, because around thirty years later I was in the same oases with a woman who is now long dead. What I remember is the woman's voice, the endless road there, the corrugated track shaking you out of the car, a low room with barely any furniture in a small inn with whitewashed walls, and then at night the unimaginable stillness of the desert, and the barking of the dogs that hung around the oasis in a circle, as if we were being surrounded by the sound. Green writes about the light, muted by the waving leaves of the date palms, and about the gentle sound of the water, and ends his sentence with "and now the German reign of terror in these indescribably peaceful places". Dates also come up in Gide, because in Tunis on February 19th he got up early to buy a kilo of date puree, all that was available per customer. There is a queue of more than two hundred people and that is too much for him, he leaves, he needs the time to write, but in his diary he does not do so until the following day, to report that the Allies have been unable to stop the retreat of Rommel, who had now rejoined the bulk of the German troops. That same day he writes that the American army has retreated, leaderless, leaving behind armoured cars, artillery and everything else, but also that the American soldiers are fighting "slowly", that they do not have the feeling of necessity that drives other nations into war, because they are not convinced of the reasons for fighting. Immediately after that, he casts doubt on the figure of 25,000 American casualties that is being mentioned, before taking an unexpectedly literary turn and talking about Fénelon and the obscurities of faith, and is dissatisfied with what he wrote in his diary a year earlier, "useless and mediocre".

And what about me, in 1943? It is the year in which my parents divorce, but for me perhaps the year of two sounds, that of the V1 that was launched near our home, a sound I did not hear again until I saw the recordings from Cape Canaveral on the television, and that other sound, so much more protracted, the *basso continuo* of British and American aeroplanes flying over to bomb German cities, accompanied by the chanting of anti-aircraft guns.

I can still hear that sound in my memory, I will never be rid of it, an orchestra of hundreds of invisible players taking possession of everything until finally it dies away, a sound bringing destiny to some other place. Two years later, my father died in a British bombing raid.

42

Last day here in the German south. Sun, but the mountains are invisible. Snow that has been on the ground for a while does not become dirty out in the countryside, it simply becomes old snow, a flat and dumb white surface without life, dead snow, a lid. The wood in the distance a black wall, nothing moving there either. Just waiting. Who is waiting? Here, I mean the trees in front of the house, but also the snow on the roof. At mysterious moments, it suddenly decides that gravity must come into play, and an enormous load comes thundering down past the window. On the roof across the road, I see a crow rooting almost scientifically among the tiles with his beak. But what is there? Something to eat, that much is clear, given his enthusiasm. But that, too, adds to the idea of a waiting room. Moles, foxes, mice, everything is waiting. If you watch for long enough, you will see it or hear it. His fellow bird, the woodpecker, tweeting away at insects to come out – it's more exciting than the internet. Later I go for a walk through the woods and hear water everywhere. The snow is melting, even if you do not see it yet, beneath the top layer, which freezes again at night, I hear the water gurgling and babbling, it wants to leave. It flows quickly alongside the path, which has itself turned into mud, where there is still frozen snow it is hard to walk. A bench stands on a curve in the sunshine, a few felled trees opposite, lying horizontally. I see how the ivy that has grown up the trunk continues to grow on the dead body of the tree, a network curling around the trunk, graceful bright-green leaves with an elegant tip, sometimes small clusters of berries, life clinging on to death. For the first time this year, I hear a buzzard's high-pitched cry, a warning to its victims, but also to me. For a while I see him far above me, turning slow, wide circles above the white landscape as if he wants to measure it. The cry means he is taking possession of it, and that I had better get used to the idea.

43

Return.

You never get used it. The last lines were about the German cold, the next ones will involve the Spanish heat. For more than half a century, I have been migrating to this island, I travel by way of France, taking detours via friends and places I have long wanted to visit, every time there is that moment when you have to surrender to Spain, but which of all the possible Spains do you choose in a country that is increasingly at risk of falling apart? I enter through the Basque Country, via Aragón, via Catalonia. Europe has been trying for half a century to become one country made up of many countries, Spain is unravelling, fleeing itself, paying the price of a centralist past, looking for former oppressed souls that call themselves nations, wanting to move away from an authoritarian era of forbidden and hidden languages, misunderstood history, tearing itself apart in an opposite movement, as a reaction to corruption and arrogance, becoming a country that no longer wishes to be a country, maybe not even a collection of countries, it no longer wants a flag but an orgy of flags, nations, characters, it is going against the tide of time, but it is no longer an *it*, not a unity, it is an anarchic kaleidoscope of possibilities, and no-one knows where it is going. And those who love this country stand on the side, watching and waiting for what is to come.

These are the days of my annual migration to the island. Car loaded up like Bulgarian Gypsies, just missing the suitcases on top, but even so luggage for four months, computers, books, clothes. We have driven via an old Carthusian monastery in the north of France, followed by dear friends in Normandy, an inn on the banks of the Vendée, the first feeling of peace, of turbulence left behind, sitting by the water and watching the opposite bank and the ducks. The next inn was by the water too, still in the French Pyrenees. A fast current, water running over pebbles, you hear the rattling of the stones all the way from your bed and you know the water there has never done anything different. You do not have that with flying, the feeling that you really are going to another country – the airport of departure looks like the airport of arrival, no customs, the same money, the same brands, only the newspaper is different, once again you find the problems of other people where you had left them behind half a year ago, division, new parties, rejection of the past, movement. You always have to surrender to Spain, you have to pass through something, an invisible border that consists of history. The mountain road I have chosen this time is narrow and rises steeply. Barely any villages, endless twists and turns, high mountains and then, almost without transition, the other system, the other language, Aragón, old land, and, as we descend, drier and more inhospitable, flocks among the cliffs, empty plains, little traffic. I know this from so much travelling, a spiritual exercise to return home to my other, Spanish life. It has never been an easy country, it gives nothing for free, I feel how it drapes itself around me, drawing me in, wanting to be conquered, and yet laying down the law. Landscapes of a fierce beauty, wide open, made for armies to move across, mountain passes, fords in rivers that have already dried up, old bridges made of enormous stones, everything smells of history, of the Iberians,

Arabs, Visigoths, Romans, who have left their genes behind in the people who belong to these landscapes. The names tell their own stories, Sos del Rey Católico, Ejea de los Caballeros, Almonacid de la Sierra. As evening falls, we see the castle of the Calatravas in Alcañiz, it lies high above the small town, the man who built it could look out over half a province, his coats of arms hang beneath the high ceiling in the dining room on banners, together with the bygone blazons and names of his vassals. Once I was here alone, at another table in the enormous room another man sat by himself, writing, we looked at each other from a distance and smiled, I have never forgotten it, it was like a reflection. Our horses were outside, the next day we would join our different armies. In the night I stand at the parapet, and of course the child that I have remained sees El Cid march by or the army of the Almohads, or Maimonides surrounded by scribes. For one who lives in writing, imagination is never far away. The next day, Alcañiz is dusty, I buy, as always, the *Heraldo de Aragón*, in which today the big news has to give way to the local news of villages and towns, Spain remains the land of the *patria chica*, the little fatherland, as it will remain even if it tears apart. I see the signs for Teruel and Zaragoza but take a back road through the Maestrazgo, wild and inhospitable, until I reach the sea, which reflects the light of the sun, the sea that will surround me all summer, not as now in its guise of a large plain, but as a harbour at the city, as a bay among tall cliffs, as the home of Poseidon and as a sound in the night.

44

The big city sends out its heralds. The traffic smokes, falters, turns into syrup.

Houses along the motorway in the black incense of lorries, the people who live there. Barcelona. When was the first time, 1954? Everything has changed, cosmopolis, nothing has changed. Through tunnels to the old harbour from where boats leave for the islands. The car in a safe place, a few hours for the city, the bookshop La Central, the crowds after the emptiness of the landscapes, as if you are an actor in the wrong play. The boat sails at night, as always, the long hour before you are allowed on board, the garage on the lower deck, the space for the car measured to the centimetre, smoke and stench, a vision of a world gone wrong. Columbus stands on his high pedestal on the roundabout, looking out towards Italy or maybe India, but he sailed in the other direction and discovered America, which was already there but did not yet have that name. Usually it is the *Zurbarán* that goes to Menorca, but this time an Italian ship, narrow corridors like a labyrinth. There is always something ghostly about the first hours, outside you see the land disappearing, lights slowly going out, the people who have no cabin sitting around televisions on which faces loom out of the mist. The poor reception at sea means that already you no longer entirely belong to the world. On deck, far below, you see the lorries lined up in battle formation, and the black water beyond, gentle waves. They used to be smaller boats, the dictator's portrait still in the lounge, later the portrait of the oh-so-young king, who is now the old king, waiters in white, or perhaps I am imagining that, still the strong smell of Spanish cigarettes that were called Ideales, the short night that seemed long, nine hours of sailing but an early trace of grey light trickling into the cabin. You peer through the porthole to see if you can make out the island, but the world is still empty, and then you head outside anyway, the men who have spent the night sitting in the *butacas* lean unshaven on the rail, dogs kept somewhere in kennels on a rear deck begin to whine and howl, the plain of the sea is misty and almost motionless, one of those strange moments when time is absent, and then, infinitely distant and vague, the first contours of the island, a drawing with the finest pencil, the outline of Punta Nati, maybe the flash of the lighthouse, the memory of earlier walks there summoning the names, like a litany in the language of the island, Punta de s'Escullar, Cap Gros, Cala dels Alocs, Illes Bledes, Cap de Cavalleria, Illa Gran d'Addaia, Cap de Favàritx, and then the wide swing past the high forts left and right, the entrance to the port of Mahón, the longest natural harbour in the Mediterranean, arrival, the city on the hill, the church like a fortress above the city, home to the other home.

45

Everything has to be reconquered, absence is a punishable offence. The papyrus has grown taller since December, so there has been a lot of rain. The leaves of the aeoniums have shrunk, they have withdrawn into themselves, are missing the high yellow towers of their winter flowers. The palms do not recognise the man who planted them so long ago, they are offended

The port of Mahón

by their injections against the Uruguayan invader, beneath the pine trees is a bed of light-brown needles, the first task. The plumbago has no flowers, neither do the new oleanders, the old one is taller and has a few. It is not a rebellion, but there is a mood. Dissatisfaction. Xec has installed a watering system, small black pipes, but they want water from people. Only the fig tree by my studio seems to have doubled in size. He needs no extra water, everywhere among those large leaves that can be used to hide so many things, I see small hard fruits, still almost two months to wait. Then I come to the last wall, the cactuses and succulents. Arnold Schwarzkopf's thick, black leaves gleam like onyx, he has struggled his way up, the tortoises can no longer reach his lower leaves. A few metres on, a miracle has occurred, a declaration of independence, the big, fat leaves of the succulent that stands there are folded even more theatrically than last year, but long, tall stems have emerged from them with, at the top, rings of bell-like flowers. I am not certain if it is a dudleya, where I bought him last year they called him cactus, which he (or she) in any case is *not*. One thing is certain, they have all survived unaided, a strong army.

The hedgehog cactus still has red spines, but there is also the beginning of a swelling on one side that will become a flower. Cactuses do not greet you, not even when they have not seen you for a long time. We stand there, just looking at each other, the one with the side arms pretending he is in Mexico, when I go and stand beside him I see that he has grown again or that I have shrunk. The other, slim, almost one-dimensional cactus, covered with weapons, is now almost translucent, and the fourth, the lonely, noble *Myrtillocactus geometrizans*, which I call the Soldier, is standing to attention as always but is not saluting. Are those their real names or am I just showing off? I have three German cactus books now, but all I know for sure is that, this year, once again, the mighty group that was already here when I came so long ago has little yellow flowers on the tips of what will become ripe fruits in September and October. They do not permit any doubt, everyone who comes here calls them cactuses, they huddle together like an army or a union meeting before a strike. Because of their height, they look down on me, I am the factory owner and they want a pay rise. They have big hands that will never play the piano, you need to keep your skin away from them, and they are reluctant to give up their fruits, their needles are almost invisible, but you can still feel them a day later. Otherwise, I live in ignorance. The cactus books are confusing, bandying about various Latin and German names for their hairy cone forms and phallic aberrations and suggestions, when I am working I know they are standing around me, the wind does not touch them, they are the most silent of residents, I live with their enigmas. They are my companions. My contemporaries have Facebook and Twitter – when I go back into the world I see them around me on trains and buses, focused on their smartphones, their flying fingers and their fleeting friends. My friends here stand still and say nothing. They are simply here.

The Soldier: Myrtillocactus geometrizans

46

My studio is not very large, but light. This is agricultural land, no building permitted, but a pigsty had once stood here, the outline of which was still visible, so the studio could be built exactly on the spot where the foundations still existed, some old stones in the stony ground, the remnants of a floor, straw-coloured dead thistles, weeds. I write in a pigsty. Pigs are intelligent animals, I hope some of their thoughts have been left behind. I have four stone walls now, the stones, longer than they are high, the kind known as *marès* here, sandstone. Natural stone, with an uneven colour and surface, it is the wall I see straight ahead of me as I write, as I am doing now, a very light sand colour. Here and there on the island are deep quarries out of which these stones were cut, sixty centimetres in breadth, thirty-three in height. The architect devised nine small windows, but I have to stand up to look outside – he did not want me to be distracted. Stendhal could draw, I remember the sketches in his autobiographical *Vie de Henri Brulard* to explain the position of something, primitive, fleeting drawings in ink, but I cannot do even that. If I could look through the wall in front of me, I would see the garden and further away the house. To the left, a big door with windows through which I can see some of the cactuses, the ficus, the fig tree, the stone wall with a narrow opening that leads to the rest of the land, where the tortoises live, who sometimes show themselves but generally do not. They live in hiding, they are probably writers, of all the animals they are the ones who most resemble writers, if only because of that shell. The trees on that piece of land are oleasters, olive trees without real fruits, they get by without me too. This winter, Xec and Mohammed took out the worst of the undergrowth, I can walk there again now. They rescued the half-wild vine that grew up the wall, for the first time there are a few bunches of grapes, the trunk, if that is what the ancient wood is called, is old and tanned, the wood looks twisted, as if it has been tortured. How is it possible that a drop of fertility can still travel through it to create those grapes? Like a centenarian, the vine clings to the stones of the wall, the light-green leaves that reach down to the red soil have been eaten away at by tortoises, wounds the shape of a tortoise's mouth. I acknowledge his Biblical heritage with a certain reverence, everything here is old, including me, and I will eat his fruits in August.

47

It is the annual ceremony, the opening of the studio. All the windows have small shutters, otherwise too many creatures get inside. I always find dried-out shells of beetles, desiccated lizards that have not survived the winter. I have tried to imagine how dark it is inside the room, but my books remain silent on that subject. After I have opened all the small shutters, I can unlock the door. It is difficult, they no longer believed I was coming, keys and locks protest but then suddenly give up their resistance, the door yields and light storms in, the first thing I see is the Library of Babel in Spanish, highlights of the fantastic literature that Borges thought we should read, all his saints, Kafka, Chesterton, Bloy, Kipling, Stevenson, Voltaire's *Micromégas*, "Lord Arthur Savile's Crime" by Oscar Wilde, the *Thousand and One Nights* according to Burton and also according to Galland, thirty-three volumes in total, all purchased thirty years ago at the Librería Católica in Mahón. Everything is as I left it in December. For six months, the books have read themselves, what I am seeing is my self-portrait as reader. And at the same time my self-portrait as a deceiver of myself, because only I know what I have not yet read. I wander in and out of my books with the whim of a man who wants it all, who can never choose, who knows that everything here has made me who I am, and that includes what I have not read. I will return to that. Like the walls, the ceiling is made of *marès*, with white beams with a slight bend, the very gentlest of triangles. The five shelves of books on the rear wall are also white, on the top shelf, standing upright in the full light from the door opposite, is a book about Dante, *The Life and Times of Dante*. He is another one I read a hundred times before really reading him. On the cover is a fresco by Domenico di Michelino from Santa Maria del Fiore in Florence. The poet stands there in crimson before Purgatory with his book in his hand, open at the first lines. The mountain of Purgatory, where you could rid yourself of the filth of your sins in an extremely slow ascent to Paradise, morality (punishment) mixed with duration (time) in a theological alchemy of the sort that medieval scholasticism was so good at. Of the Dutch names for Purgatory, *Vagevuur* is the most beautiful. Together with *Voorgeborchte*, or limbo, which must be somewhere in its spiritual vicinity, it is among the most beautiful words in the Dutch language. Dante would have been shocked had he known the Church would do away not only with the word, but also with the idea, *rien ne va plus*. Another place we can no longer visit, but in the fresco – and therefore on that cover – it still exists. Bowed under an invisible lash, the naked sinners trudge upwards in circles, in the poem, too, they move extremely slowly, Heaven has to be earned. The poet does not see them, he has already written them. He stands there motionless with his back towards them, his outstretched right hand pointing at nothing in particular, the book in his left hand, face contemplative, laurel wreath around a beret-like hat the colour of dried blood. The entrance to Purgatory is narrow, there is a moral geography at work here that is not explicitly visible in the painting. First comes the Ante-Purgatory, where souls must remain endlessly in the waiting room, Cantos 1 to 9, and then, in Purgatory proper (Cantos 10 to 27), the seven deadly sins are dealt with in a sequence that would no longer apply these days, with the proud having to do most penance, and even though they are spirits who want to ascend, they are physically punished in their bodies, which no longer exist, a malignant miracle in itself. No body, and yet pain. All kinds of things are taking place on these seven terraces of the mountain, those who on Earth suffered from that peculiar form of melancholy known in the Middle Ages as *acedia* are perhaps the ones who are sitting and lying around, later it seems as if the souls who still resemble people are starting to run, and right up at the top of the mountain is the divine forest of Paradise, the reason why all this began. At the end of all those rhyming three-line verses, in which six hundred people appear, and which the exiled poet worked on for all those years until his death, he will look into a light that will blind him, a mystical *visio Dei* – he can only stammer when he tries to describe it, but no-one in literature has ever stammered more beautifully. In Kurt Flasch's wonderful *Einladung, Dante zu lesen*, the geography of Heaven, Hell and Purgatory is described as if you could travel there. For Dante, the Devil was indeed a spiritual being, but one who, when ejected from heaven, had left a funnel-shaped crater in the earth like a meteorite: a hole that would become hell, the place through which the man in the picture passed with Virgil, from layer to layer. In the waters of the southern hemisphere, the empty rear side of the world, the mass of earth released on that impact became the mountain we call Purgatory, lying at a point directly underneath Jerusalem, a high and lonely rock in an endless sea. Odysseus once tried to sail there and was swallowed by the waves, along with his friends. That, too, is in Dante. Why did Odysseus have to die? Because his journey was forbidden. Is that why he was in hell? No, that was because of the Trojan Horse. Deceit was another sin. So, did Odysseus never return to Ithaca? Or had Dante not read the *Odyssey*?

48

I put the book back in its place, and the poet looks into my studio from there. There is such an infinite amount of world in the fresco that it is as if the small room I am in is filled with the power of the imagination, quite literally. Suddenly it seems as if all those books descend from that one Book, or as if they know one another in some mysterious way in an anachronistic whirlpool in which Brodsky is of course related to Joyce and obviously to Homer and Eliot too, everyone has visited Dante's universe, just as Dante himself has walked in and out of Virgil's world, everywhere you suspect secret and not so secret family connections and wandering genes, but before my delusions of reference run away with me, I notice the painted portrait directly beneath the image of Dante, a man who can himself see no-one because he has closed his eyes. Without knowing it, they were contemporaries – almost, in any case, but the poet from Florence would have recognised the meditative pose, the man wearing a sort of monk's habit sits in the fork of a tree, his head is shaved, his hands are together, on a branch beside him hangs a censer, which is also recognisable, only the trees are different, they are eastern trees, they have fine leaves and needles, lightly drawn with ink and water, liana-like growths are wrapped around the tree, on the ground below are strange sandals with high wooden blocks, in the sky two small birds that look just like birds, even for Dante, the man would not be an extra-terrestrial and yet he is not of this world, he looks inwards and we cannot see what is to be seen there. Maybe, without being aware of it, I once also looked the same when Mstislav Rostropovich played Bach's cello suites from the pulpit of the Nieuwe Kerk in Amsterdam. Years ago, I saw that drawing for the first time at Kōzan-ji, a small monastery temple outside Kyoto, and in the years since I have returned to it time and again. There were hardly ever any other visitors, the print hangs in a light, airy room that opens onto a garden, you can sit on the top step of the stairs leading out there, a pond, stones covered in moss, trees the colours of autumn, and, when you turn around, that likeness in which the man sits just as still as ever, he has not moved in the intervening years, I am the only one who has moved. His name was Myōe, he lived from 1173 to 1232, he was a learned monk of the esoteric Shingon school of Buddhism, and he founded that monastery. I am not a religious man, but I like to sit in that garden, even though it is a little far. That is why I have brought Myōe here, Dante and Myōe, two masters, one looking, the other with his eyes closed, together they watch over Baudelaire, Kierkegaard, Yeats and Montale, Parmenides and Proust and all those others who spend the winter here. They get along excellently. Shingon teaches that we are already enlightened without knowing it, a reassuring thought. If you gaze for long enough into the mystery of the world, you will be blinded, and that involves a lot of light. What Dante saw at the end of his *Divina Commedia* was so much light that he could not really talk about it. The eloquence of that silence is encapsulated in the last four lines of his poem, which appear to have been written with that light. It was a long journey full of terrors, hell, purgatory, heaven, a tidal wave of successive three-lined rhyming verses, a poem like a sea. It begins on Good Friday 1300 and ends seven days later. He wrote the first words in 1308, the last in 1320, a year before his death. Seven days, twelve years, fourteen thousand two hundred and thirty-three lines, a hundred songs, one poem. Words that have occupied people for about seven hundred years now. Certain people.

49

Some of the visitors who come here have two feet, a few have four, and there are those who have more, but they have wings too. A few of the four-legged ones can run straight up a wall, they usually arrive in the evening after dinner and want something to eat. Nearly everyone here has a standing appointment, and if I want to see them, I have to keep that appointment. This has to do with moments, with who comes when. Carmen, for example, arrives on Wednesdays at nine, to help Simone. Xec and Mohammed come when there is something wrong with the trees or the plants. Last week they hung strange plastic objects in the pine trees that are meant to combat the plague of processionary caterpillars on the island. I had seen what looked like a dangerous nest on one of the higher branches, but it was not clear how any creature might get in or out of it. It still isn't, because my suggestion of getting rid of it was received with a mild form of disdain. The disaster had either already occurred or would not, the small, cone-shaped sculpture hanging in the tree, which those invisible creatures had apparently worked on for so long, had become an ornament, no longer representing any danger, and the plastic bags that had now been suspended up there would ward off any danger. I had already seen the bags dangling here and there on the island, gracefully moving in the wind, particularly when they caught the sunlight as they swung, they seemed more like an adornment than a trap, which is in fact what they are. Something is concealed within, a scent I cannot smell, a temptation I cannot feel, but it is designed to seduce the moths to lay their eggs right there, so that the larvae are born in captivity. Maybe that point has not yet come, but the nest high above sways threateningly in the wind today, and the plastic bags, which have some kind of black belt at the bottom that has nothing to do with judo, hang low enough for me to see that there is no creature inside them yet.

The processionary caterpillar. Once upon a time, as a boy, I walked in processions, but we did not look like those caterpillars, or at least we were not attached to one another, and those caterpillars are. A photograph on the internet shows a long line of hairy creatures, all connected. In the photograph they are standing still, but you can tell from the picture that they are advancing, slowly and threateningly, those hairs, which are defensive stinging bristles, can inflict wounds, they have barbs, together they form a hairy snake from a horror film. Their mother, if you can put it that way, is a moth, and like the invader who has it in for our palms, she is a moth of considerable beauty, that strange shade of light brown that is actually grey, a colour used only for couture that is still made by hand, and that is what the *Thaumetopoea* looks like. *Thauma* means miracle, and *poea* has the same root as *poiéo*, which not only means "to make" in general, but also to make poetry. So, my enemies' mother is a poet, but I can't quite get my head around that idea – Anneke Brassinga, Neeltje Maria Min, Elma van Haren do not fit the image. My caterpillar, then, is a creator, a maker of miracles, and yet her lines mean misfortune for my pine tree, that much is certain. I need to think some more about the word *pijnboom* too, if only because Dutch is the one language in which a pine tree is also a pain tree.

50

And the other appointments? One is with myself. Very early in the morning, I sit out on the terrace before the sun gets too hot. This is the hottest summer I have ever experienced, and that is what everyone is saying here. I have been coming to the island since 1965, when I was thirty-two. Tomorrow I will be eighty-two, and I have not missed a year, so we are talking about fifty years, sufficient for a small statistical study. I myself think I have simply become less able to bear the heat. I certainly do not undertake the long walks of the past in the hottest part of the day, and in the mornings it is quiet and cool. Hours before that, you are slowly woken by a landscape of sounds that belong to the realm of sleep. As soon as the first of the neighbours' roosters start crowing, interwoven with the accompanying noise of the hens, the donkey, too, begins to bray, tearing the night apart, all the dreams of his night are in his passionate roaring, it is daytime, there is no going back. Then I hear the geese belonging to a more distant neighbour, a sound between panic and protest, no wonder the Romans used them to guard the Capitol. That sound, too, is part of the appointment, the day is a clock. Late in the evening, the bougainvillea gets his water. He stands against the white-washed wall of the house in his own territory, and at this early hour the water has not entirely dried up. An insect approaches it, one I have not yet been able to place. Nabokov was a lepidopterist, Ernst Jünger knew all about beetles, and I know nothing, that much has become clear to me here. At first I thought it was two attached to each other, which seemed tricky when it came to flying, but that is not the case, he, as I will call him for the sake of convenience, consists of two parts, with a corset of invisibility between them. By that I mean that his rear end looks like the continuation of his front end, but with a transparent interruption. I can't work out what he is after, but there must be something, because he comes every day, and exactly on time, hovers, with some apparent sense of purpose, just above the ground, which is still a little shiny and beginning to dry, lands now and then, but I can't see if he eats anything, and he can't actually be drinking either. His double black shape hangs above what must look to him like a desert at the hour of dew. Is there something minuscule there that makes him fly here every day? For want of a better word, I call him (or her?) the Two-in-One or the Binity, because like the Trinity, he poses theological puzzles. Even more puzzling at that hour are a number of extremely small insects, mosquitoes that are not mosquitoes, who have an equally strange obsession but later in the day have vanished. It is perhaps shameful that I do not know their names either, but since I recently read a book by a Swedish writer who lived for a year on an island between Sweden and Finland and discovered and described 640 different moths, I have forgiven myself a lot. But these are not moths. Small though they are, they have conceived a perverse love for the old table that stands in a corner of our terrace.

What is it? They hover at the edge, keeping themselves in balance with their essentially invisible wings, through a curious thermal dance that seems to serve no other purpose than to remain near that table. The table was once painted – is that it? Are they addicted to the smell? Do they sniff it? By now I know that everyone here eats everyone else, a dead bird does not lie around for more than five minutes before the ants arrive, but paint? Robots and insects are our future, but I understand some insects better than others, even though I do not know their names. Another two, then. The first one is like a torpedo.

He comes in the evening and flies with the fathomless precision of a fighter pilot (like a Messerschmitt, I wanted to say, because I am a child of the war) into the deep-purple flowers of the bougainvillea. He is pointed, a rather aggressive shape that you would not expect of someone who takes the sweetness out of flowers. I am more fond of the second one, who is like a bumble bee but is not a bumble bee, because he has no fuzz. One day someone will come along and teach me everything. He has a distinguished black sheen and is in love with two flowers that Simone puts in big pots at the edge of the garden every year, the *Gaura lindheimeri*, a flower at the end of an endlessly long thin stem that arches high into the air. The end of endless – is that possible? No, it is not, but that is where the flower is, in one of those shades of red for which no-one has ever come up with a real name, and that is the flower he wants. What happens next is a miracle of acrobatics, because as soon as he sits inside the flower, his weight drags down the stem, an almost untenable position that he maintains for as long as possible, it is only when gravity forces him to let go that the stem sweeps back up again, flower and all. I do not know where he goes with all his sweetness, but he will be back again tomorrow. And me? Just after I had written all this, I saw the tortoise, no, one of the tortoises, because I cannot always tell them apart, walking along the wall towards the grapevine. Slowly, of course, so I could see it clearly. I did not lose sight of him until he disappeared into the vine leaves, but I thought nothing of it at first. Green leaves, I thought, let him enjoy them. He stayed there for a long time, and I went to look. A bunch of grapes hung beneath the lowest leaves. He had already started on the grapes at the bottom. Everyone here eats everyone and everything, but those grapes were mine. Suddenly I became a part of everyone and everything. I saw that he was right, the grapes were ripe, and I should pick them.

51

My books stand upright against the back wall. Those are the books that are always there, classics, works of reference, Frazer's *Golden Bough*, Diderot, the Bible, Saint-Simon, everything you can wander into and out of. Then there are the other books, which are connected to my various obsessions, or to a subject I am working on, or would like to be working on. They are on tables and in a large bookcase. Those are the horizontal books, they lie there according to a specific strategy that is not always conscious but can still be valid even after a year of absence. When I come back to the island and have not yet unpacked the new books, I see the ones from the previous year and sometimes they are arranged in such a way that I cannot help but remember what I was planning to do with them. Leopardi's *Zibaldone*, a lofty mountain I have wanted to climb ever since I visited the house of the lonely hunchbacked count in Recanati. He wrote one of the most beautiful poems in the history of the world, but last year I shied away from his *Zibaldone*, over two thousand pages of his notes translated into English. He can wait, and so can I. But why did I put that volume of Borges down so emphatically, with that piece of paper between two pages? And what is Max Frisch's diary doing at such a conspicuous angle on top of Humboldt, who is hidden inside a case? It is a book from the Bibliothek Suhrkamp, white, with that familiar stripe a third of the way up the cover, the sign by which you can always recognise this library of wonders. I open the Borges book at the page with the piece of paper sticking out. It is about history, and I am immediately back home. With Borges, as with Kafka, you can always be certain that after just a few lines a thought will come along that you cannot ignore. Something sticks, you have to pause, you have to read it again.

The essay is called "The Modesty of History", and you're already off, if that same day you have read a newspaper full of Greece and ISIS and hundreds of drowned refugees, then history is not modest, and yet what does Borges write? "A Chinese prose writer has noted that the unicorn, precisely because it is so unusual, will pass unnoticed. Our eyes see what they are used to seeing. Tacitus barely noticed the Crucifixion, even though it is recorded in his book." You read that sentence and, when you are two lines further on, it draws you back. The man who was crucified there divided history into two parts, the time before him and the time after him, but in Tacitus' *Historiae* the importance of his death went unnoticed. We live in an age when the history of what happens is written down every day. What do we miss amidst everything we do not want to miss? Borges continues: "I was prompted to this reflection by a sentence I stumbled upon by chance when leafing through a history of Greek literature and was intrigued by its somewhat enigmatic character. It was the following sentence: 'He brought in a second actor.' I paused, saw that Aeschylus was the subject of this mysterious act and that this, as can be read in Chapter 4 of Aristotle's *Poetica*, took the number of actors from one to two." Before continuing with Borges, I will make a marginal comment. Of course it was not "by chance" that Borges happened upon that sentence. It happened because he was most likely not reading the book by chance at all, no more than it is because of chance that here in my studio I have a copy of Aristotle's *Poetica* in an old Penguin edition – *Aristotle, Horace, Longinus, Classical Literary Criticism*, because I brought it here years ago, not at all by chance, to use a quote from Longinus for my book *The Following Story*. In that sense, chance does not exist.

When the crowd in Athens five hundred years before Christ (see above) suddenly saw a second person on the stage of what Borges calls the "honey-coloured theatre", it must have been a huge shock. Aristotle describes it in a sober – one might say "modest" – way, he simply says that Aeschylus was the first to increase the number of actors from one to two, but that is precisely what is so revolutionary, going from one to two, because that meant introducing the dialogue. Everything that was subsequently added was no longer a revolution. Sophocles came up with three actors "and painted scenery". After that, nothing happened that was not to be expected. In Shakespeare's *Hamlet*, the two have become twenty-four, including Francisco, a soldier; two clowns; gravediggers; Reynaldo, servant to Polonius; supplemented by a whole crowd of nameless lords, ladies, officers, soldiers, sailors, messengers, attendants, the miraculous multiplication of actors. That was the revolution, but I do not know if it can be categorised as modesty. A man on a cross, a governor washing his hands, the first actor for the first time made to say something to a second actor by the man who has written their words, and what about us? What is happening that we do not see, what have we not understood? The Higgs boson? Here I am on dangerous ground, where the mysteries of reality are greater than I can comprehend. That must be why Leon Lederman, who to the fury of other physicists called the Higgs boson the "God particle", asked the question in which all modesty has disappeared: "If the universe is the answer, what is the question?"

52

I hurry back to the world I know, the world of appointments. Before dinner, when I sit outside on the terrace, a flock of pigeons rises from a distant farm. They must be homing pigeons, around eight is the time when they are released, an aerial ballet. I cannot count how many there are, they are moving too quickly. They seem to be looking for their positions, from where I am sitting there does not appear to be any obvious leader, they do everything at exactly the same time, turn to the right, disappear, come back again, drop down, climb high, vanish behind the trees and come back one last time before disappearing for good. The best moment is when, during a sudden turn, they catch the late sunlight in their wings, for one moment they are made of purest gold, and they seem to stand still for just an instant. I cannot imagine that they are not happy in their high-speed ballet.

I do not need a clock for all of this, everyone knows their own timetable, they have drummed it into us. And no-one skips a day. The neighbours' donkey, for instance, who every evening, when we have eaten on the terrace and switched on the Spanish news at nine, trots across his field, loudly braying, and waits behind the wall until he gets his daily carrot. Simone has to reach over the wall, he grabs it between his big teeth, I will know until the day I die what it sounds like when a donkey eats a large carrot. Less than an hour later, after darkness has fallen, I spot the first gecko. He emerges from the wall around the terrace, pretending to be invisible, a miniature dinosaur against the white of the wall. He does not have camouflage. I see his little feet and those strange toes with which he defies verticality, I know he thinks I cannot see him when he is standing still, and yet that is when he is at his most visible. If I as much as lift my hand, he is gone in a flash. Then he hides behind the blue terrace door, which is wide open. That is the moment when the other one arrives, usually from the roof. Both of them are on their way to the lamp that lights up the terrace from behind a semi-circular roof tile. I do not know what their relationship is, sometimes the one chases the other away, on other evenings it is as if they hunt together. The only hierarchy I can detect is that the smaller one always gives way to the larger one. There is no visible command, it must be a minuscule shift in the big one's position. You see the small one cautiously moving closer, both heads focused on the spot where a moth might land. Then suddenly there must have been that signal: you are surplus to requirements. And the smaller one skulks away, but I know he is never entirely gone, and so does the bigger one. They can sit perfectly still for ever, and that is how mosquitoes and moths are caught. The moment of danger. An almost transparent moth has been attracted by the light, which blinds her, and has settled for a second on the blue of the doorframe, I see one of the two geckos standing still and then moving forward with extremely minimal steps until the lightning-fast attack happens, which must have been mathematically calculated so that mosquito or moth has no chance. This is also the hour when the scops owl makes his metronomic sound and, like me, waits for the count of four until he receives an answer from afar, and the hunt can begin. Everyone is eating everyone else, and I am going to bed.

53

No, Max Frisch's diary was not just lying around for no reason. Reading with imagination has to do with series. I still remember where I got stuck last year, and I look the passage up. Frisch uses different fonts in his diary, so some things stand out more. After a page of italics (246), suddenly at the bottom something almost like a typewriter font. I have travelled a lot in Japan, so the first sentences of the first paragraph are familiar. "Japan, November 1969. What am I doing at five o'clock in the morning on a boulevard in Tokyo? The little workers with yellow helmets in the bright light of the welding equipment. No fruit. The temptation to think that when people are small they are also naive." *No fruit* so abruptly there in the middle of the paragraph is in itself peculiar, but what do I mean by series? That my thoughts are at once no longer in Japan, but with the new Spanish king, before jumping to the political tensions in the country where I am now, Spain. The king is about two metres tall, even taller than his father, Juan Carlos. This is particularly noticeable when he travels to South or Central America, as the former colonial power's head of state, for the inauguration of yet another new president. Everyone is smaller, sometimes much smaller. At times I feel it physically when I look at the photographs of those encounters. The king cannot stoop too much, that would be awkward. The president has to look up. We may assume that the king does not think, in Frisch's sense, that the person standing there beside him is naive. But still. In two bodies there is at that moment a tension that I would not immediately wish to compare to that of my two geckos, but there is an unspoken physical relationship in which politics, history and power relations are not permitted to play a role and yet are present. This is even clearer in what is happening now in Spain. The king is at a football match, standing beside Artur Mas, the president of Catalonia, of which he is still king, and when the national anthem is played, he is booed and whistled. He and Mas both act as if they cannot hear it – but they can. Mas, who is not very short, but still shorter than the king, is sawing the legs out from under the throne. Not long after that, the new mayor of Barcelona had the portrait of the old king removed from the council chamber without replacing it with a photograph of the king who was booed at, and at a meeting of radical *Independentistas* his photograph was actually burned. Yellow and red flames, the yellow and red flag of Spain and the yellow and red flag of Catalonia, same colours, different arrangement. In Barcelona, many of those flags hang on balconies, but the Catalans themselves are also fiercely divided. An intense back and forth in newspapers, on the radio, television and at demonstrations. The central playing on legality, saying that this is strictly about elections, not about a referendum on independence, but the unspoken question behind that must be: what are they going to do if on September 27th the people choose the parties that are in favour of a farewell from Spain? Will they send in the army? Language plays an important part in all of this, so the situation on the islands, where a slightly different form of Catalan is spoken, is closely followed. Mahón should be called by its Catalan name, Maó, once again, and the new female mayor has had the Spanish flag removed from the tourist train that runs along the harbour in the summer, one of those silly little trains full of well-fed English and German tourists looking like eleven-year-old children with Alzheimer's. There was a lot of laughing about it here, but no-one is sure that it is really funny anymore, just as the Catalans are unsure about how they will deal with the division sown by Mas. A land torn in two as a new member of the EU. No sooner has it been united than the continent begins to fall apart at the seams.

54

And the garden? And the silence? I have kept the world at a distance, but I have not fallen off it, not yet. The formation of a crack, whether it is happening to Spain or to Europe, can perhaps be heard even better in silence. I have walked out of my studio to fetch coffee. The heat today is indecent. The heat, that is how every conversation begins here, the ritual Introit of every Mass. *Mucho calor hoy*, says Carmen. I agree and say that we often spend the first two months of the year in the south of Germany, where it always snows and freezes then, sometimes minus 10 or 15. She takes note of the forty or fifty degrees difference between now and then and says "the human body can cope with anything", and there is nothing you can add to that. As I walk back with my coffee, I see, on the other side of the wall, the donkey standing in the middle of his bare field, looking at me. The hair around his eyes is lighter in colour, so it looks as if he is wearing a mask or peering at me through a pair of hairy glasses. The force of his gaze stops me in my tracks, and he does not move either, just stands there motionless, and looks.

55

Frisch quotes Gorky on Tolstoy, but he actually intends it for Brecht, about whom he is writing in his diary. The sentence is as follows: "In spite of the one-sidedness of his Doctrine, this fairy-tale man has an infinite number of sides." I would be more inclined to find Tolstoy fairy-tale than Brecht, but the circumstances make the sentence easier to understand. Two playwrights, one from the extremely comfortable confederation that did not experience the war, the other, who spent the war as a Communist in capitalist America and has returned to the Marxist, Russian-occupied part of torn and conquered Germany and now leads the Berliner Ensemble in East Berlin. But the diary from 1966 actually begins in 1947 in Zurich, because Frisch does not write down his memories until nineteen years later. Brecht, back in Europe for the first time after all those years of exile in America, is staying in Zurich with the dramaturge of the Schauspielhaus. He has not yet returned to Germany, but at least here in Switzerland he is already back in the language. Frisch is at that time still working as an architect. He has already written a couple of plays, without great success, which will not arrive until 1958 with *Biedermann und die Brandstifter*. The great novels, *Stiller*, *Homo Faber*, *Gantenbein*, have not yet been published. Between them, there are thirteen years and the war that bypassed Switzerland. Frisch tells Brecht about his visit to the destroyed Berlin, Brecht listens and then says: "Perhaps one day you will find yourself in the interesting position of someone talking to you about your fatherland, and you will listen as if you were being told about some region in Africa."

The quote from Gorky above tells us that Frisch thought Brecht was "fairy-tale", but I think the core of the quote should be sought more in that "In spite of the one-sidedness of his Doctrine". The fairy-tale element is not evident in the description. You feel the younger man's respect and distance. You read for the first time that the older man can be open with him when they visit one of Frisch's construction projects together for the first time, and he expresses his respect: "*Alle Achtung, Frisch, alle Achtung!*" And when they part company after that, the farewell is explicitly "collegial". What Brecht thinks of Frisch as a writer is less obvious at that point.

In 1948, Frisch is there when Brecht sets foot on German soil again for the first time, in Konstanz. They have driven there in an old Lancia that belongs to someone who works at the theatre, but as they approach the barrier, Brecht says he wants to cross the border on foot. They walk about a hundred metres, then Brecht stops, relights his ever-present cigar, looks into the air and says: "The sky's no different here." An architect who is also a writer, to this we owe a comment by Frisch when he later meets Brecht in poor, bombed-out East Berlin. The villa where Brecht then lives is not wrecked, only the garden is neglected, the architect in Frisch sees that the house is spacious, but there are hardly any carpets. Frisch sleeps in a former maid's room, he feels that the conversations with Brecht are different here in East Berlin from the ones they had in Zurich, but he also says he cannot prove that. He notices that Brecht has completely changed the *haut bourgeois* interior of that villa without rebuilding, he did not have to "defend himself against the architecture, Brecht was stronger, and it did not function as in a confiscation or even a change of ownership; the question of who owned the villa did not come up, Brecht used it as the living always use the buildings of the extinct, the course of history." Frisch, who is not a Marxist, relates this without commentary, but in that *course of history* you can hear the Marxist echo of the *inevitable course*, an article of faith that can also turn against you in an ironic or dramatic way. Whether that was the case on 17 June 1953 with the workers' uprising in the DDR does not concern Frisch when he writes his diary much later, but it must have crossed his mind when he saw those photographs of Russian tanks. Maybe someone can find out what happened to that villa after 1989. They see each other one more time, in 1955, in Chausseestrasse this time. Frisch writes about it: "He looked old, sick, his movements were sparing." Lunch happens "*ziemlich wortlos*", with few words. At a certain point the word *Wiedervereinigung*, reunification, comes up, and Brecht says: "Reunification means emigration again." Later he asks Frisch what people in the West think about the danger of war, and Frisch notes that the people who come from the West now come from a very long way away. Anyone who has never crossed that distance of just a few kilometres cannot imagine what it was like. He had come from a rehearsal in West Berlin, where Brecht's daughter, Hanne Hiob, was acting in a play Frisch himself had written, but he does not say which one. The isolation had become almost total, in the most essential way, these were two separate worlds, and anyone who, like Brecht, believed in that one world had to live that belief every day, alongside those others who did not – or had ceased to – believe in it. I visited the house on Chausseestrasse when the Wall had already fallen but the DDR still existed. You still had to cross the border at Bahnhof Friedrichstrasse. Thorough checks, different money, when you came out the air was different. No-one believes it anymore, but that is how it was. It would be some time before the separate history was patched up, inadequately and temporarily, in the form of a shared currency. I do not remember much about the house, but all the more about the nearby cemetery. *Lommerrijk*, shady, leafy, that is how you might describe such a cemetery, and I see now in my *Roads to Berlin* that I did indeed use that word, a curious sort of consistency after twenty-five years.

I walked around there for a while, from Brecht's grave to Hegel's, from Hegel to Fichte and back to the defaced grave of Brecht, who lies there with Helene Weigel. Fichte and Hegel also lie with their women. There were anti-Semitic slogans sprayed on Brecht's grave, but I had already seen them that morning in the newspaper. So Brecht was still alive; that much was clear – as long as people insult you, you are present. Hegel cannot have read Brecht, but of course Brecht had Hegel in his bloodstream via Marx. Perhaps that was why in my story back then I was overcome by a wild fantasy between those two graves, the thought of everything those two men had written, what they had scribbled into the world until it changed. "Suddenly I felt as though all those words were literally lying beneath my feet, a gigantic, interwoven construction, mineshafts full of songs and paragraphs, the words of one, so much more accessible, dancing around the granite system of the other, a dual kingdom running rampant beneath the other graves, where *Surabaya Johnny* rules together with the World Spirit, Mack the Knife dances in Bill's Tanzhaus in Bilbao with *Phänomenologie* in his arms, and a ship with eight sails steals dialectics away to a coast where soldiers are changing the guard for the last time and marching to the beat of the disappearing State."

What strikes me now, when reading his diary, is how good

Frisch is at observing what, for someone else, would be minor details or trivialities. Several times he returns to Brecht's neck, once in 1948 that neck is "naked", later, in Berlin, it comes back again: "Above all, the neck, so naked." Writers are peculiar people, there is, in that diary at least, no fundamental discussion between Brecht and Frisch, perhaps in reality, but not explicitly in writing. Everything is in the descriptions. I have looked at photographs of that neck, but I could not see what Frisch had seen. I see only the familiar, iconic face, the rather small eyes behind the round glasses, the neck of a man in his fifties. And yet a whole world emerges from just a few pages of diary. The system of the DDR had become the prevailing reality of the theory, a reality that a writer from Switzerland could step in and out of, which was impossible for most writers from the DDR. There was, even before the Wall, clearly a here and a there. The last visit was in Chausseestrasse, in a room with a view of the cemetery where Brecht would lie not long afterwards. Frisch: "I have met few people one would recognise as great, and if someone were to ask how you could actually see the greatness of Brecht, I would not quite know what to say: actually it was always the same: no sooner had you left him than he was more present, his greatness worked in retrospect, always a little belatedly, like an echo."

56

I met Frisch only once, in Edinburgh. What do I remember about it? Not a lot.

Mulisch, Reve and I formed the Dutch delegation at a big writers' congress.

1962. Four years before he would begin that diary. He was not a large man, and he wore a pair of glasses with a thick frame and what looked like double lenses, so it appeared as if his eyes were magnified. I was twenty-nine, and he could not have read the only work of mine that had been translated. But you are present, so maybe you matter. Not much of Harry's work had been translated by then either, but he had his allure, and he radiated an infinite sense of security. We stood with Frisch at the bar, what we spoke about has vanished. Frisch had had a few, was enjoying himself, and he let us talk. Harry cut through the crowd with that nose like a figurehead, and maybe Frisch made a note of that. There is always something exciting about encounters with writers you cannot read, because there is nothing to prove. Henry Miller was walking around, Angus Wilson, Stephen Spender, Norman Mailer, famous Scots we had never heard of, you belong but you are nobody and God knows what you have written in that strange language of yours, and everyone is friendly. I felt like one of those innocent children in Limbo, never yet sinned, waiting for heaven, which might be a hell. One image has remained with me. In a room where all those celebrities were wandering about, there was a noble Scottish family in kilts with the colours and tartan of their clan. They wore shoes with silver buckles and daggers with silver hilts tucked into their woollen knee socks. Dinner jackets above their skirts, gleaming black bow ties, insignia.

They did not so much as glance at these possible celebrities, if they even recognised them. They sat there like atavistic statues in a feudal oasis, being served from behind by people who did not look at them, and were completely sufficient unto themselves. It is half a century ago, and still I remember.

57

Like the Netherlands, Switzerland shares a border with Germany, but they speak German in a part of Switzerland, while in the Netherlands they do not. Although we – or some of us – are known there, we do not in essence belong. We might just as well be Portuguese writers or come from Guatemala. But what exactly is the position of a Swiss writer in Germany? Sometimes, like Frisch, they are published in Germany, while also, because of their Swiss themes, remaining outsiders. What does that mean for Swiss writers? Are they a part of German literature or not? But a German writer never becomes a part of Swiss literature. There are local problems, peculiarities and intimacies of which they are unaware. For Frisch's generation, there was also another issue. Switzerland had stayed out of the war, they had no shared past of persecution or neutrality, of right or wrong, exile or not. And yet, for a Swiss writer, that large neighbouring country, with its powerful language, was a constant challenge and presence. The big German newspapers reviewed their books, the major theatres put on Frisch's and Dürrenmatt's plays. Now and then

you heard something about their rivalry, gossip is an insep-
arable part of every literature, every country has its "big two"
or its "big three", there is always a Szymborska who wins the
Nobel Prize and a Zbigniew Herbert who does not. At the
Théâtre de France in Paris, I saw Frisch's *Triptych*, in which
the dead mingle with the living, and Dürrenmatt's *Der Besuch
der alten Dame*, which, probably completely incorrectly, I
could not help thinking of as a Godot in reverse, one that
required no waiting, one that simply came, with all its tragic
consequences. I had not seen *Die Physiker*, but read it, enough
to be briefly startled when, after a reading in German, in the
Francophone part of Switzerland, a tall, imposing woman
came up to me and introduced herself as Charlotte Kerr, while
also making it clear that she was Dürrenmatt's widow. She
offered to give me a lift back to my hotel. This happened at
considerable speed in a red open-top sports car. On the way
there, she spoke about Dürrenmatt, about his books and also
about his paintings and drawings, and then she asked if I had
time the next day to come and take a look. I did, and so
that sunny day we drove up a high hill to a large house with
a magnificent view over a lake and a valley below, a Swiss
postcard, that is how I remember it, together with the curious
scene for one lady and one gentleman that was acted out there.
When we were inside, she asked me to accompany her to
Friedrich's study. It was spacious and light, I see mainly lots
of windows, a huge desk with a view of the lake below, and
a large, almost menacing, gleaming black chair. I looked at the
art on the wall, but I no longer remember it. The chair, that
was what it was about, because at a certain point she said:

"Wouldn't you like to sit in his chair for a moment?" Tall, slim, and in my memory a redhead, she stood beside me, and I said that I would rather not. She took note, lingered a little longer, said she would leave me on my own for a while, and pointed again at the chair.

Now the room was not only empty, but also quiet. The more I looked at the chair, the more certain I was that I did not want to sit in it. It was *his* chair. From photographs, I knew that in later years he had had a rather impressive build, which was probably connected to the impressive size of the chair. I stood for a while in the bright light of that room, thinking about how he had sat there alone and written, a form of being alone that comes with writing and that irrevocably creeps into the bones even of bad writers, and then I left the room in search of my hostess. The house was spacious and empty, she was waiting for me in another light-filled room with a glass of champagne and a salmon canapé and she asked: "Did you sit in his chair?" and I said that I had not, to which she replied that she understood, and a little later she took me back to my hotel.

58

For the first time in two months, rain. I watch the small tortoise scuttling past to an unknown destination, he looks as if he has a goal. The rain makes the yellow and green of his shell gleam, the green becomes darker, the yellow lights up, as he walks across the red soil like a piece of jewellery designed by no-one. I'm not exactly sure what cactuses think about

The Mexican

The martyr

rain. The big cactus, the one I call the Mexican, has endured heavy winter rains in my absence, he can handle it. But the phallic one has belted in his waist in recent months as if holding his breath in some terrible way, and the martyr, the one with the spines on every side, seems to be consuming himself from within, a revolutionary without an enemy. And the really big one, one who is several, although I don't know if you can put it that way, is being washed. Some of his big fat hands had curled up in recent weeks, as if the heat had afflicted them with a plant form of arthritis. The slim leaves of the oleaster that stands beside and above him had dropped into his creases and dried up, he stood with his hands full of faded detritus, which is now being rinsed away. In a month's time, his fruits will be ripe. They are called *chumbas*, our old neighbour, Bartolomé, now long dead, always came to fetch them for his pigs. Bright green at first, later a dry and ascetic shade of yellow, within a few weeks orange. Inside, full of a voluptuous pulp with hard seeds, which produces a delicious tropical juice. The French call the fruits *figues de Barbarie*, otherwise known as prickly pears. You can only take hold of them using tongs, which is also the only way to peel them if you do not want your hands to be covered in the extremely sharp needles, which can be almost invisible. I do not know what pigs' tongues and palates are made of, but Bartolomé's pigs were apparently up to the challenge. Palate – *Gehemelte*? Such things happen when you have been living outside your language for a long time, when that language is not around you on all sides. I had written it down, but the word suddenly became a puzzle. Sometimes, unexpectedly, you no longer

The original inhabitant

remember a word, and today that word is *gehemelte*, the daily Spanish has made some of the words of my own language more mysterious. Sometimes it is because such a word contains another word that means something itself. *Hemel*. Sky or heaven. *Gehemelte*. Palate, roof of the mouth. Yesterday it was *gevest*. I wanted to describe that Scottish family's daggers, and at that moment the word, in English *hilt*, was no longer there. I sat there for a moment, very still, wondering if this was old age. It was not *handvat*, handle. *Gevest*, my memory claimed out of nowhere, but I could not believe it and said the word out loud. *Gevest*. It did not sound at all right. *Gehemelte*. *Gevest*. Filled with doubt, I headed for my Van Dale dictionary, and there it was. It is sometimes even stranger when it comes to expressions that you suddenly lose trust in because you are not sure where they came from, such as when my German translator, with her unrelenting logic, asked me about the Dutch expression "spijkers op laag water zoeken" (literally, to look for nails at low tide), which means "to find fault, to split hairs". Her question was: but wouldn't it be much more difficult to look for nails at *high* tide?

59

Germany, the large country. It lies there in the middle of our weary continent and struggles with its density, its past, which, almost everywhere, is also that of others. Germany has nine neighbours, each with its own past and present, with which the German past and present is intertwined. There is a French present, a Greek present, a Hungarian present, and it refuses to truly become a European present, if only because there is also a German present that contradicts itself within Europe. A nice drawing by Eva Vázquez in *El País* of July 10th, a month ago. You should always leave newspapers lying around for a while, to see if they remain valid. The picture accompanies an article by Timothy Garton Ash with the simple title "What is at stake", but it actually says it all by itself. On a grey surface, most likely a tabletop, there is a large, blue matchbox. The box is open, there is only one match left inside. On the top of the box there is a ring of alternating red and white, which no doubt represents a lifebuoy. On the table, a large number of curling, half-burnt matches. No sign of a new box. Garton Ash is clear and says what we already know but cannot hear often enough: the continued inability to really do something about the crisis is not just about weak Greek and inconsistent German leadership, but also has to do with the international and European institutions. He holds two people responsible: Andreotti and Mitterrand, two, as he calls them, old foxes, who, immediately after the fall of the Wall, forced Kohl to set up a timetable (*un calendario* – I am reading the article in Spanish) for European monetary union. They knew they could not stop German reunification, *Wiedervereinigung*, and they demanded the currency as the price. When all that was going on, a French invitation to a European conference arrived and I was allowed to go along as a small cog among a number of Dutch heavyweights, including the psychologist Nico Frijda and the historian Maarten Brands. It took place in Prague in Hradčany, at the castle above the city, and a rumour went around that this was an attempt by Mitterrand to prevent the unification of Germany. I do not remember if all those implications really dawned on me back then, just as I no longer remember where we slept. The castle and the strange crowd gathered there meant that my mind was more on Kafka, and I was fascinated by the city and its German, Jewish and Czech past and the bridge over the Vltava with all those Baroque statues. Not long before, I had received the Légion d'Honneur, and Brands and Frijda were winding me up about it and suggested I should take this opportunity to thank the president personally. I was too much of a coward, and the others were making fun of me a little. It was all teasing of the kind that students do, something of which I have little experience, but when Mitterrand walked through the room after his speech and came to the spot where we were standing, they gave me a hard shove in the back and I ended up practically at the feet of the president, who turned out to be strangely small, the usual small-to-large distortion that television can create. I mumbled my thanks for the distinction, which he most likely knew little about, but he shook my hand and said: "C'est naturel, monsieur." What I remember is the sphinx-like appearance of his face, a dry, white skin, eyes taking you in from a distance, probably weighing you up, the extremely chill tone of his voice and the enigma of his words. Because what exactly was it that was "natural"? That I had received the honour, or that I had thanked him for it? For a moment, I was at the French court, but no sun was shining. I do not know whether anything political was achieved at that conference, maybe it was only intended as a signal to Germany, that at least is how some people interpreted it. And now? Germany is still where it is,

Greece, following a wild period of *opera buffa*, is still attached to Europe. The handsome minister on the motorbike has vanished into the wings, from where he continues to argue his case, and we laypeople feel as if we must choose, but between what? Between two economic theories? Between two kinds of Europe? Between governments and rebellious parliaments? Reason and populism? But behind every singer is another chorus of economists singing through the arias, here the composer has tried to make the cacophonic crack that runs throughout Europe clearly heard. Continue soft-soaping with a last-minute reprieve every time, with a choir of goddesses of vengeance in the background, or in spite of all the lamentations of nostalgic sovereignty, correct the original error and create a real community, which seems more inconceivable with each passing day?

60

Woken from my first sleep. The high-pitched cries of curlews. Sound carries a long way here, curlews live on the coast, but do not often allow themselves to be seen. You hear them in the late evening, sometimes at first light. A piercing sound that takes a run-up and then winds itself up a few times. *Grielen*, curlews. In the illustration, long legs, yellow. The iris in the big eye is bright yellow too, with a black pupil. Gone from the Netherlands as a breeding bird. Its nest a simple hollow. When there is trouble, it presses itself to the ground. Hunts at night. A bird after my own heart.

I find it hard to get back to sleep. Later in the night, I wake again. The heat is still lingering, I go out onto the balcony and see Orion. His stars are incredibly bright, they sparkle, holes in the darkness. Unlike in the north, the great hunter lies on his side here, just above the neighbours' holm oak. No light anywhere. The sea is close, there is no wind, it must be wonderful to be sailing out there now. The world seems far away, but I know there are people travelling across this sea, there are pictures every day, a man on a Greek island holding his child above a churning crowd, police no longer able to put a stop to that vortex of furious bodies, coffins with bodies, people floating in the sea. And on the other side of the continent, men trying to climb over high fences to enter the Channel Tunnel. History here is not modest, this part of the world is changing its character for ever, we are becoming different people as we stand here, we just do not see it yet, but perhaps that is precisely what Borges meant by modesty. *Il faut cultiver notre jardin*, that other writer said. I do my best, but my garden is in the world, whether I like it or not. Curlews and Orion on the one hand, bodies floating in the water and men jumping onto moving lorries on the other.

An image from the realm of the absurd comes to mind, I do not resist it, it is already there.

Once upon a time, a street in Zamora. The guidebook says that the nuns in Convent X make a special sort of biscuit. I am not that keen on biscuits, but I am curious. There are still women who voluntarily live together behind bars in the middle of a city. When you report to the convent, a hatch opens up. What you feel and smell is convent, a place of cyclical time. Everything always happens there at the same time, every day the same eternal bell, which goes on chiming when one of those women departs. What I see is a white face looking at me from behind stern glasses; what she sees is the world in the form of my face, maybe also the street behind me. It is a quick transaction, something else opens up beneath that hatch, a tray. I deposit my money in it, receive the virginally packaged biscuits. It is no more than that. But when I watch the television in the evening, it is I who looks out at the world, and I am the nun.

61

Repetition of moves. Greece is once again veiled behind a political lie, this is not going to work and everyone knows it, Europe is broken before it was truly whole, the German parliament is staging an expensive and sad charade in order to look better in the history books and the Dutch parliament is hypocritically dancing after it, in post-Maoist China the stock exchange of the pseudo-communist party is making the world's capitalist stock exchanges shake and Spain continues, unabated, to tear itself up in a half-hearted attempt to settle the very old scores of a corrupt and arrogant centralism. My garden is not really bothered about it all, its inhabitants have different concerns, which are to do with wind and water. Astrologically, the sun has left my sign of Leo without a farewell letter, the dog days are over, the three cat days come creeping in as if they have spotted a bird, a phenomenal storm has sent grey casemates of cloud surging ahead with an almost unbearable threat, and when the storm finally arrived, after all that mugginess, and the rain stood vertical on the land, part of my wall collapsed. It looks like an open wound, as if someone is walking around bleeding, with his insides on the outside. Red is the colour of blood, and the interior of the walls here consists of smaller stones that still have red soil on them, and when the wall gives way under the pressure of the storm and the water, within moments the path outside is blocked by a manganese-red mass, the large light-grey stones on the outside have fallen furthest, the next morning Xec and Mohammed come and, like surgeons, put the body of the wall back together again. Before seven, I hear one of the oldest sounds in existence, metal on stone, a repeated and melodious tapping to get the large stones back into a shape that will allow them to fit together without cement, the secret of the *pared seca*, the drystone wall, the emblem of these islands. But first the innards have to be put back in their place, stone intestines, stomachs, hearts, everything is gently arranged until the large stones that once – goodness knows how long ago – were hacked out of the ground here are placed as a protection around the little ones, and the wall once again looks like a wall. As they are already here, Mohammed clips the dry, drooping leaves of the yucca so that all the daggers are pointing up at the sky again. I tell him that one of the four crowns finally started blooming this year, a lofty tower of white flowers appearing among the daggers, the white unfurling begins at the base of the tower, when the blossoms above are still hard and green, but within one week the beauty rises up to where the light comes from, shines for a few days and starts work on a memento mori, a brown and shrivelled anti-flower that I would like to excise right away because I have got the message. If you want to think about decay, there is nothing quite as eloquent as a garden that immediately provides the antidote: in another spot it is claiming something else entirely, as there is an abundance of figs this year, Carmen went home with a full basket, and the fruits on the big hand-cactus are beginning to flush.

62

Repetition of moves (2). The mystery of the Binity – see 50 – has been solved. In the hall is an ancient triangular cabinet. It has two doors with small windows, with glasses inside. Yesterday I saw the Binity hovering in the air in front of it. He was working away at something in a corner where a piece of wood had broken off. It was not clear what he was doing, but he made a high-pitched humming noise as he did it, a little as if someone was working with a very fine and lyrical dentist's drill. As I approached, he flew away, dancing, in an irregular sinking and rising movement that looked like large footsteps in the air. What I saw was a minuscule construction, a mysteriously round shape of the kind you see in paintings by Hieronymus Bosch. It was so perfectly round that you almost expected to see a house number on it, a Euclidean mud-coloured form, which is why I had not noticed it before in the broken-off wood. Suddenly I understood what he had been looking for in the mud at the foot of the bougainvillea in the mornings. This was about a nest, so maybe the Binity was in fact a female. Or do the males make the nests, and would the other half come along later? The question is: Do you leave it there or not? Does the Binity have a sting? How many immigrants can we allow, and how many offspring will be coming to live there? And what are they supposed to do when we lock up the house and leave, and they become prey for the geckos that live behind the shutters? Will there be a revolt of the spiders? You think you have a dilemma, but you do not. You are no match for the mysterious ways of the Binity. Front, invisible mid-section, black slightly bulbous rear end has chosen *this* place and no other, will not allow itself to be chased away and builds a new nest, two metres away, flying back and forth with invisibly small lumps of mud that are stuck to the white wall. I am getting to know her better and better now, as she sometimes sits still for a moment while she attaches her clay to the wall. Do not disturb! The high notes of her Gregorian chant lead me to a new theological insight. Maybe that invisible midriff is the Holy Spirit? She builds and builds and does not stop, and I have no book in which I can find her worldly name. Cactus books, butterfly books, tree books, I need different indices for her. Mohammed, who never comes inside and is now sitting outside on the ground with his lunch, leaning against the wall, which is now whole again, cannot help me, and besides, he did enough yesterday by knocking the processionary caterpillars' nest, which I could not reach, out of the pine tree with a long stick. It looked like the shrunken and withered long-haired skulls from Mexico or Peru that I once saw in a museum. They were skulls of real people, with little mouths that were once able to speak, and that was what was so gruesome about it. Everyone has a right to eternal rest, and that does not involve being gaped

The Binity

at in a display case by people who live a thousand years after you. Fortunately, at least they had their eyes shut.

63

I will remain with skulls for a moment because in the Spanish newspaper there are three of them, depicted against a black background. They do not resemble those prepared miniature skulls of real people in any way, nor do they look like the pensive skulls of meditating saints in the paintings of Zurbarán or Hieronymus Bosch. They show a rising trend of evolution, the first is little more than a roughly sculpted block of stone, full of cracks and fissures, the second, *Australopithecus*, has been obligingly placed in the photographer's light and therefore looks more elegant, and only then do we come to *Homo habilis*, still very dead and turned to stone, but at least approaching our likeness. Ancestors, I understand from the clearly written article, which races through evolution and then, for the sake of simplicity, proposes starting from scratch again, because two major palaeontologists, Jeffrey Schwartz and Ian Tattersall, have just done so, in order, as they put it, to show the luxurious diversity of our ancestors. Six million years ago (so many autumns gone by) we and the chimpanzees were still the same thing (*cosa*), but shortly after that we split into two branches. Our branch began to develop towards *Australopithecus*, with a skull volume equal to that of the chimpanzee, half a litre (rounded off). That is what the article says in Spanish, litre and rounded off. We are liquid. Two million years ago, it adds, the liquid inside our skulls increased to a litre. Which is better for thinking. And by two hundred thousand years ago, it was one and a half litres, and then the article says, "and that is when what we call history began". So here I am with my inherited luxurious diversity and my one and a half litres, and I read that Tattersall believes that the palaeontologists of the past two centuries saw everything incorrectly and that the luxurious ("*lujuriante*") diversity is the reality, one that does not entirely correspond to the existing theory. But what then? One of my dictionaries does not have an entry for *lujuriante*, but it does give the old medieval sin of *lujuria*: "lust, lechery, lewdness". The thicker dictionary, Van Goor, says for *lujuriante* "engaging in fornication, very opulent". So, the new theory about our origins is opulent, because Tattersall is unlikely to mean fornication. What he does mean is that every animal – and that includes us – is a mixture of ancestral and modern traits. "Everyone has inherited traits from a whole series of ancestors, from the very oldest to the most modern, we have teeth, but fish have them too, we have five fingers, but so do crocodiles, and seven cervical vertebrae, just like giraffes and rats. What is important in determining the species of human are the features that only a few species have in common. And this has not yet been properly researched." And there I am with my one and a half litres of brains, my fish teeth, crocodile fingers and rat vertebrae, and I read in Montaigne in another context, but equally valid here: "When a new doctrine presents itself, we have every reason to be on our guard and to remember that before its appearance the opposite was fashionable. And just as this theory is overthrown by the second one, a third theory may emerge in the future, which will similarly discredit the second one." And, as always, he underlines his opinion with a quote from the classics, here Lucretius, with the natural and calm assumption that his readers could read Latin:

Sic volvenda aetas commutat tempora rerum:
Quod fuit in pretio, fit nullo denique honore;
Porro aliud succedit, et e contemptibus exit,
Inque dies magis appetitur, floretque repertum
Laudibus, et miro est mortales inter honore.

"Thus it is
That rolling ages change the times of things:
What erst was of a price, becomes at last
A discard of no honour; whilst another
Succeeds to glory, issuing from contempt,
And day by day is sought for more and more,
And, when 'tis found, doth flower in men's praise,
Objects of wondrous honour."
(Lucretius, *On the Nature of Things*, V, 1275–80)

64

Try staying away from the world, and the world will catch up with you. One day you see two pictures of a man with a child. One is leaning slightly forward, near a lot of water. He is wearing a uniform and those big soldier's shoes that we used to call *kistjes*, boxes, and he is carrying a child in his arms. All you can see of the child is its little legs and feet. It is so small that someone else must have put the shoes on those feet. You know at once that it is dead, you can tell from the man's face. The man is sad, but it is not sadness for himself, it is sadness for the child, for the bankruptcy of the world. The day before, I wrote about Bosch, the book was still open on the table, at the picture of a famous painting by him that hangs in Rotterdam. St Christopher. The story is well known. A heathen giant, Reprobus, finds a child on the banks of a river and realises that it wants to get to the other side. He lifts it onto his shoulders and wades to the opposite bank. On the way, the child becomes heavier and heavier, so heavy he can barely lift it. It is Christ as a child. Since then, the man has been known as Christopher, the Christ-carrier. He is the protector of all travellers. In the painting, Christopher has the same stance as the policeman on the Turkish beach, leaning slightly forward, with great care he is carrying the child to the riverbank, where it will be safe. He is looking to the right out of the painting, just as the man in the newspaper has his face to the right, where we are, but it is as if that child is also too heavy, and this is true, because death weighs heavily. The child was too heavy for Europe. Europe does not exist, so it could not lift that child.

65

There are forms of longing so absurd that we should come up with another word for them, if only to expose the associated lie. And yet. When, as I did on the evenings before last week's big storm, I sit here looking at the moon like a German romantic from the time of Hölderlin and imagine that people really once walked up there, I don't call that longing. I don't need to go there, and certainly not wearing such an idiotic suit. No, I mean something else when I talk about my lie-infected longing. This is about a stupid machine that landed somewhere on a rocky, dusty, grey field, where you can almost touch the gravelly stones. What is it precisely? The complete lack of humans? The dominance of the mineral? The absence of anything that might resemble a plant, no matter how monstrous? We do not belong there, and yet we are there – is that it? So, would I like to go there? To all those swirling mists and gases and craters with their damaged faces? The machine is still transmitting, I know all about its long journey, its light years and the nonsensical procession of zeroes trailing after all those impossible numbers like some insane bridal veil. I look on the internet at the planet Pluto and its moon Charon. Pluto is Hades, the god of the underworld. Poseidon is a more beautiful word than Neptune, Hades a heavier sound than Pluto, a name already contaminated because of its association with money. With that name, Hades can be the god of the underworld, although his realm feels like an infinite upper world to me, a region that Charon, who is his moon, may never visit. Charon is the man who sails in Patinir's boat between heaven and hell. The painting hangs in the Prado, I have seen it many times. On the left, the landscape is still paradisiacal, somewhere on a green hill an angel has spread its wings ecstatically, ready to take off, but Charon is rowing and does not look, he is busy rowing to a darker world. The small, pale soul sitting in the front of his boat is illuminated by a ray of light shining from whence they came, I hear the sound of the single oar as they sail past the other bank, where it is dark. Fires burn in the hills, black smoke hangs over the water, they must be sailing to the strange round building with the semi-circular dark entrance, the gate to the house of Hades, the final destination of the increasingly ethereal soul, unless Charon were to row onwards, over the edge of the painting.

66

And me with my longing? What was I trying to say? I know it was an eleven-year-old girl who gave Pluto its name, a child. That is allowed, u and o are sounds for children, they would never choose Hades, the word sounds too harsh. I use the internet to ease my longing, a photograph taken (things can take photographs, everything can be done without humans) seven hours after *New Horizons* came closest to Pluto. Seven hours, 360,000 kilometres away. Here the machine is given a human face, because the text says: "He looked back for a moment." Through the window in the back of the car, through the rear-view mirror? You can picture him doing it. And what does he see? The perfect curve of Pluto's silhouette, clasped in a silver ring made by the nebulae that hang above the planet. Perhaps I do not know myself what I mean by longing, but the thought that there are actual mists above the planet enchants me, as does the photograph of the planet itself.

Perhaps it is because of the solitude of those objects hanging there so detached in space. In one of the photographs, you can see Pluto, light beige with a dark patch here and there. The background is an intensely black expanse by Rothko and there, further away, in the top right corner of that rectangle, hangs Charon, who has just taken that soul away. He is round now, almost transparent, he no longer has to row. Another picture zooms in on Pluto. Craters, an ice flow of nitrogen, I look at it as if it were a map – and I want to walk there. A small rucksack, a notebook, I have studied the map in my travel guide, the peaks of the Norgay Montes, then further on the Sputnik Planum, where the heart of Pluto is located, and bottom left, at least four hundred miles away – though I do not see any roads – is the Cthulhu Regio. Many of my journeys have been to names, Isfahan, Ithaca, Atacama, and now I want to know: does the wind blow in the Cthulhu Regio? Will I be able to hear the ice as I walk there? What sort of clothes should I take? And those mists, will their light reach the Earth? My footsteps think earth, but what did Neil Armstrong think? In which year of my endless absence will someone walk on Mars?

67

Once you have been in space, you do not get away from it that easily. Because of a book I was writing, I once visited the Smithsonian Institution in Washington and, as a result, I have developed a special connection with the Voyagers. *Voyager 1* and *Voyager 2*, two travellers who have been moving through space since 1977 and, in the four or so decades that they have been travelling, have been forgotten by just about everyone except NASA and me. Whenever I heard something about them, I thought of Herman Mussert, who was my protagonist and who, like me, had visited the Smithsonian Institution.

Whether he, like me, has continued to follow their progress, I do not know. The book, which is called *The Following Story*, was published in 1992 and on the last page my hero Herman Mussert died, and the dead do not exactly tell us much. As for me, I find I am still unable to let go of them. On 9 July 1979 at 22:29 UTC, *Voyager 2*, launched on 20 August 1977, flew past Jupiter at a distance of 570,000 kilometres, on 25 August 1981 at 03:24:05 it passed Saturn, and on 24 January 1986 Uranus, and finally on 25 August 1989, at a distance of 4,950 km, Neptune, and all that time I have gone on living, eating, travelling and writing, while the lonely voyager moved through the universe and sent its messages. On 19 December 1979, *Voyager 1* caught up with *Voyager 2*, but no-one was talking about that in the Amsterdam bars I visit when I am in the city, and there was no talk about it in Berlin or on this island either. By then, 2 had discovered a few rings around Jupiter, and the big red spot they talked about in space-travel circles turned out to be a complicated storm moving anticlockwise. But the most important thing was that 2 had seen that there were active volcanoes on the moon Io. Poor Io! She was once the priestess of Zeus's wife, Hera. Zeus fell in love with Io and, according to some accounts, Hera became jealous and transformed her into a heifer, guarded by the many-eyed Argus. A bewitched heifer as a moon of Jupiter, something doesn't quite add up there. Hermes, the protector of travellers, did his duty and killed Argus, so Hera sent a gadfly to chase the detested Io, which Io constantly had to flee, and since then the former priestess has turned her eternal circles around Zeus, who as a celestial body is known as Jupiter. In a space photograph from 1979, the relationships become clear. Io, pursued by the gadfly, hangs like a small golden pearl under the massive spotted marble body of her fateful lover, Jupiter. That was where we were when I wrote my book and Herman Mussert visited the Smithsonian in Washington, a Latin teacher fired for a relationship with a student, who says of himself:

Obviously space is our destiny, that much I concede – I live there myself. But the excitement of the great voyages of discovery will pass me by [. . .] I belong to the past, to the time before Armstrong put his big, corrugated footstep on the face of the moon. That was another thing I got to see that afternoon, for without thinking anything in particular I had drifted into a sort of theatre where there was a film about space travel. I found myself sitting in one of those American swivel chairs that hug you like a womb, and set off on my journey through space. Almost immediately tears sprang to my eyes. [. . .] Emotion ought to be inspired by art, and here I was being misled by reality, some technical wizard had worked optical magic to strew the lunar gravel at our feet, so that it was just as if we ourselves were standing on the moon and walking around. In the distance shone (!) the unimaginable planet Earth. How could there ever have been a Homer or Ovid to write about the fate of gods and men, on that ethereal, silvery, floating disc? I could smell the dead dust at my feet, I saw the puffs of moon-powder whirl upward and settle again. I was divested of my being and no substitute was in the offing. Whether the humans all about me were having the same sensation I do not know. It was deathly quiet, we were on the moon and yet we would never get there, in a while we would step outside into the shrill daylight and go our separate ways on a disc no bigger than a guilder, a free-floating object adrift somewhere in the black drapery of space. [. . .] Off went the *Voyager*, a futile, man-made machine, a gleaming spider in empty space, wafting past lifeless planets, where sorrow had never existed except perhaps for the pain of rocks groaning under an unbearable burden of ice, and I wept. The *Voyager* sailed away from us into eternity, emitting a bleep every now and then and taking photographs of all those gelid or fiery but ever lifeless spheres which, together with the orb we must live on, revolve round a flaming bubble of gas; and the amplifiers, standing invisibly around us in the dark theatre, sprayed us with sound in a desperate attempt to corrupt the silence of the solitary metallic voyager. A compelling, velvety voice began speaking, at first making itself heard through the music, then as a solo instrument. In ninety thousand years' time, the voice intoned, the *Voyager* would have reached the outer limits of our galaxy. There was a pause, the music swelled like toxic surf, and fell silent again to allow the voice to fire a parting shot: "And then, maybe, we will know the answer to those eternal questions."

The humanoids in the theatre cringed.

"Is there anyone out there?"

All around me it was as quiet now as in the deserted streets of the universe across which the *Voyager* hurtled noiselessly, bathed in a cosmic glow, and only in the fifth of its ninety thousand years. Ninety thousand! By that time the ashes of the ashes of our ashes would long since have disowned our provenance. We had never been there! The music gathered momentum [. . .]. The voice gave forth one final burst: "Are we all alone?"[4]

68

Other than in the world of science fiction, the answer is still yes. We are alone in space. Perhaps my longing is connected to that. Here, on the north coast of the island, is a wild rocky basalt-coloured area around a deserted lighthouse called

4 From Ina Rilke's translation of *The Following Story* (London: Harvill Press, 1994)

Favàritx. After last week's big storm, a kind of small lake has formed, and that stops you thinking about space. But usually it is dry and without vegetation. Black lumps lie scattered here and there, and on some days when the light is as sharp as in NASA's photographs, you can easily imagine a space probe there, an alien metal object that not only takes photographs, but is also photographed. I can look for ever at space photographs, perhaps it is because of that one time at the Smithsonian, when we stood with our feet in the moon dust, as that is something I will never forget. It is because of all those photographs that we now know what planets look like. What you want next is the impossible. To walk there, and suddenly to be startled by a lizard or a rat among all those rocks. Not far from me is the Isla del Aire, "the Island of the Air". You used to be able to row there in half an hour. I don't think that is allowed anymore. When it was allowed, I went ashore there. A path, arid scrub, thistles, stones and dust all around. There, too, a lighthouse that is uninhabited but still gives light, there are days when the Mediterranean is dangerous. Three thousand refugees have drowned in it this year. If they were ever stranded on that island, they would encounter black lizards, found only in that place, which is less than three dozen hectares in size. A hallucinating drowning person might think he had landed on an asteroid.

All he would hear would be the wind and the waves, the rustling of the grasshoppers and lizards.

69

By now, Shakespeare and mythology are running out of names to keep up with all the Voyagers' discoveries and images: Cordelia, Puck, Ophelia and Cressida are moons of Uranus, the black-and-white Iapetus, long known but never before seen in this way, and the bruised, affronted Mimas, prowl their eternal circles around Saturn like panthers in a cage of gravity. I do not know who is listening, but the Voyagers still talk to us and will continue to do so when we are no longer here. On 15 September 2013, the *National Geographic* announced the big news: on 25 August 2012, *Voyager 1* had left the solar system and become the first human-made object to enter interstellar space. There, on the edge of the solar system, the solar wind turns into an interstellar wind, in a hostile region that contains the leftover debris from thousands of exploded stars in our Milky Way, or as the *National Geographic* put it: "The solar wind flows outward from the sun traveling at one million miles (1.6 million kilometers) an hour, a bath of energetic particles that's blasted off the solar surface and into space, where it surrounds our star like a bubble." Between the one wind and the other, the wind of the solar system and the wind of interstellar space, lies an area that has not yet been named, and after that it becomes so complicated that I hang my head and retreat to my garden. One day someone will come and tell me all about it, and I will listen like a child to a fairy tale.

The suffering hibiscus has a bud. After two weeks of my watering it and talking to it, the tubercular child has shown a sign that it wants to live. There is no Settembrini nearby, I am not Thomas Mann, so no more will come of it than these few lines, but still. Persistence pays off. Bare, sorry branches. The two other neighbouring plants, bought later, have died, but they were clearly not of the same kind, so no mourning. He was one of two. At the beginning of the summer, Simone could no longer bear to look at it and transferred the second one, also beginning to resemble Chopin at the end of his suffering, into a pot. (Cornel Wilde's blood on the white keys of the piano, never forgotten.) I wanted to keep the first one, thereafter known as mine, alive. Simone's, in a sheltered corner beside the large cactuses, had flower after flower. Mine went on sulking, pulled a last-will-and-testament face, followed by a deathbed face, and seemed to want to take revenge on something. Just now I am reading Helen Macdonald's excellent book on hawks (*H is for Hawk*), and she, within her own book, reads the tragic book by T. H. White, who, like her, attempts to train a hawk to hunt, but fails miserably owing to a fatal lack of insight into himself and the hawk, and so that love turns to hate. Was ours a similar situation? No, I persisted stubbornly, but with love. And today the first bud, after an entire summer. Was it the storm and the huge flood? Does Nature always know better? It is still a puny plant with a dwarf-like stature, but it raises that one flower in the air like a flag, or as a poet might hold up his first successful poem. I do not know when cactuses who do not live indoors are supposed to bloom. Do they fertilise themselves or are bees involved? I do not know if there is a season for that either, and neither do I know anyone here on the island who could tell me. Because that is this month's second secret: the one that is close to the ground, etched with deep grooves and crowned with red stalks, which I think is called *Ferocactus*, suddenly has four flowers after the rains, without any help from me. For two years he has stood behind my studio, an unmoving, deadly silent danger zone, and now this. Ochre mixed with orange, and then on the top of the clenched bud an extra, minuscule bright-yellow star, flower upon flower. It is as if a monk has given birth to a child, and I do mean a monk, not a nun. In 1929, Karel Čapek, the Czech writer who is said to have added the word "robot" to our dictionaries, wrote a small book about the gardener's year, which contains a short but hilarious chapter about cactus lovers and the insane theories of their different sects.

Central to this story is an absurd conversation between three fanatical enthusiasts, the kind of piece that could have been written only by someone from that part of Europe. Kafka was also a Czech, after all. "What's the best soil? Does the water really need to be at 23.789° C?" "No, no, you have to water your cactus every two days with sterilised water, using 0.111111 grams of water per square centimetre of soil, preferably half a degree warmer than the surrounding air."

My monk has done all this himself, without asking any questions or saying anything to me, he has, as slowly as a tortoise, given birth to a colourful set of quadruplets between his spines.

The hedgehog cactus

71

Night. I am where I was. Back on the island. Winter. Orion directly above the garden, 23:20. I have been out into the world, bombings, refugees, in this country elections that have solved nothing. The tragicomedy of Artur Mas, no Euripides but Aristophanes, or not even that. Four parties, and the Spanish character that seeks oppositions, in Spain there are no polders, no processes of discussion and consensus. And in the Netherlands two ruling parties who are trying to learn the lessons of the chameleon, how do you turn from a socialist into something for which there is as yet no name, and how do you move from liberal to populist? With the refugee as *deus ex machina*, the one who changes the landscape for ever, the future compatriot.

I never meant for this to become a diary, I wanted to go inwards, and to stop going outwards. I had been out there for so long, and so often. The feeling that I have been removed from it, from my time. With a firm hand. The Dutch *leeftijd* – its constituents "life-time", its meaning "age" – is an ambiguous word. Time takes its irrevocable course, but life changes and wishes to make peace with its ending. There is nothing melodramatic about this, and the garden is instructive. This is a strange summer in the winter. Two months of absence, the phallus cactus has split at one of its seams, I gaze into the wound and think it will heal, I can put my fingers inside it, I am an undoubting Thomas. Two of the succulents have purple flowers, as if it is a party. Xec has reduced the oleaster at the side of the house to its main branches, a skeleton. In the city, the harbour is empty, almost everything is closed. The nights are more silent than ever. Drove to the sea tonight, stood there for a long time and listened. Two months ago, from the deck of the *Zurbarán*, I saw the island disappearing. I watched it wearing away, first the recognisable features, a group of rocks off the coast, a village, a bay, a lighthouse. Later nothing, or the nearly nothing that still wants to say something, outlines, land as a form of mist, after that truly nothing, a black dance of infinite slowness, the slowest of rises and falls, the breathing of a planet. Now I have to get used to my other life once again, the constant transition.

72

Augustine, I read, would open the Bible at a random page, as if it might tell him what to do or think at that moment. The Romans did the same with Virgil. I try it, Book VI of the *Aeneid*, and I find myself at an elm, *ulmus opaca*, a huge tree that provides a lot of shade. This tree has old arms, with empty dreams, *somnia vana*, beneath every leaf. I see the tree before me, it looks like my bella sombra in the corner of the garden, at this hour invisible and itself a sombre dream, one I do not wish to dream tonight. I read the cadence of the lines, the trap of terror, Aeneas in the darkness facing a three-bodied giant, harpies, monsters, but when he attacks them and slashes into them with his sword, it all turns out to be fake, hollow figures of nothing, an enemy made of shadow, and as if it is meant to be, I hear the neighbours' distant geese, who, woken by some noise or other, are having their own nightmares.

73

The first day of the year, the night here was without fireworks, a black velvet hood over everything, more than ever the feeling that the island is a ship sailing through the night.

Took a book from the shelf, Mallarmé, not looked at it in years, afraid of that cold marble, the sculpted perfection. Some poems you read, others you stare at before you begin to read. I read the grave sonnets for Poe and Baudelaire, but stare first at the rhyme scheme of the tercets: a, a, b – c, b, c, then try it out loud, it sounds like a cross between staccato and swell, on a ship once again. At the back of the book, a brief biography, and within that, in the year 1866 – when he is twenty-four – an excerpt from what is clearly a letter, although it does not say to whom.

He has been working for a long time on what should have been a play, his *Hérodiade*, and then declares: "Working away at the poem until this point, I suddenly faced two abysses that make me despair. One is the Void, where I arrived without knowing anything about Buddhism, and I am still too miserable even to believe in my poetry and to return to the work that I put aside because of this devastating thought. Yes, I *know*, we are nothing but empty forms of matter and yet sublime because we have invented God and our souls."

The image of the poet facing the abyss brought to mind an irreverent quote sometimes attributed to Groucho Marx: "We were standing at the edge of the abyss, but we've taken a step forward." But that is exactly what Mallarmé did, a step that lasted first two years, and then his entire life. After those first two years, in 1868, he wrote to François Coppée: "As for me, it has been two years since I committed the sin of seeing Dream in its ideal nakedness [. . .] and now, having arrived at the vision of pure poetry, I have almost lost my mind." And a month later, he wrote to Eugène Lefébure, with whom he was living when he faced his first abyss: "Certainly, I have returned from the Absolute [. . .] but dealing with it for two years has marked me, a sign out of which I would like to make a *sacre* . . ." *Sacre*, accession to the throne, anointing of a king, holy celebration. *Le Sacre du Printemps*. The word is not easy to interpret, when I add in Stravinsky's music, I see a large fire, an auto-da-fé, the fire in which heretics died, what Mallarmé was looking for was a poetry that would express the absolute, however that might be defined, a poetry stripped of all that was superfluous, everything that had congealed around it over the centuries, the vast and inescapable legacy of the past. I can only compare it to Malevich or Mondrian. There was a good reason why various people left the auditorium when the *Sacre* was performed for the first time in Paris in 1913. Those sounds did not yet exist, the ears to hear them had yet to be created. One year after his crisis, Mallarmé read Descartes, and a year after that he delved into the secrets of linguistics. You can perhaps cast off the ballast of art, but not so easily the ballast of language, since you cannot abolish the language you use to write. The language itself is its own ballast, an inheritance of ancient words from thousands of vanished mouths that have come to occupy our own. No-one has ever fallen silent, they are all still participating in our conversations: parents, ancestors, soldiers, farmers, beggars, priests, prostitutes, soothsayers.

74

The bella sombra shakes out his leaves as if they are infested with mites, and the strong wind has broken off a palm branch. At the market, Segundina, who I buy our fruit and vegetables from, talks about this summer in the winter, she is happy about it, and yet uneasy. In the island's *Diario* she has read that it is two degrees above zero at the North Pole, while in other winters it has been minus 40 – that does not bode well, as if disaster is slowly creeping up on us. While we were not here, there was a huge storm, she says, it was lethal, some of the bella sombras on the square above the harbour, behind the market, have snapped or blown over. Have I seen the damage yet? No, so I go there and find myself on a battlefield full of the casualties of war. The bella sombra is not a strong tree, it is full of water, they are huge, they are giants, yet vulnerable. They have all been drastically amputated, there is hardly anything left of two of them. Their fearsome elephants' feet are still planted in the pavement, they raise the stumps of their severed arms into the air in a manner reminiscent of Zadkine's statue in Rotterdam, these are casualties of war, but not yet dead. Small green leaves are already sprouting from the sawn-off limbs, on that square they have become their own contradiction, it will be a long time before they provide shade once again. The one in my garden has held up well. I humbly sweep away his dead leaves and feel the urge to thank him. If he had blown down, he would have taken half the wall with him, and that is not allowed, I am counting on him surviving me. I tell him as much, and as usual I do not know if he has heard me.

75

What is absolute poetry? In the same year Mallarmé is standing before his fateful abyss, he writes a poem called "Brise marine", "Sea Breeze", a poem that would have appealed to the romantic Slauerhoff. It is not yet the pared-down writing that he later envisioned, here the poet himself is still present, sensitive, here the language has not yet ousted the meaning. The autonomous construction that must have been hovering before him and that he would think about for the rest of his life remains a distant shadow, the task impossible for now. Here, the poet wants only to get away, out onto the sea, to go with the sailors, to break free from his life:

> *Un Ennui, désolé par les cruels espoirs,*
> *Croit encore à l'adieu suprême des mouchoirs!*
> *Et, peut-être, les mâts, invitant les orages,*
> *Sont-ils de ceux qu'un vent penche sur les naufrages*
> *Perdus, sans mâts, sans mâts, ni fertiles îlots . . .*
> *Mais, ô mon coeur, entends le chant des matelots!*

76

How do you get via David Bowie (back) to Gombrowicz? The first has just died, and the second does not want to leave me alone either. This morning, in *El País*, various photographs of Bowie, a different man every time, someone who constantly wanted to be someone else, who did not want to commit himself to one identity. In the *Corriere della Sera*, Cardinal Ravasi tweeting a few lines from 1969's "Space Oddity":

"Ground Control to Major Tom . . ." and the Vatican's newspaper reporting that Bowie was "never banal". Last night, a film about five important years of his life, in which he said he did not actually want to be anyone, that they were only roles that he played. So, as far as the cardinal is concerned, he succeeded. Gombrowicz's eternal obsession was with "immaturity", the possibility of not having to be anyone yet, not having to have a *definitive* form. István Eörsi, in his *Tage mit Gombrowicz* (1997), puts it like this: "The hero of his book *Ferdydurke* is disgusted by the 'mature' forms into which he is supposed to grow inevitably, those of school, of the enlightened bourgeois family, and of the conservative landed gentry. [. . .] Gombrowicz's longing for immaturity, which lasted until his death, is at the same time mourning for lost youth."

In the images I saw in the film yesterday, something similar was going on. Time seemed to have no hold on Bowie, a man who is constantly someone else for other people cannot grow old as himself, so it is almost as if you do not know who actually died yesterday. The first recordings were from the early 1970s, the last from 1983, and as the years passed he seemed to become ever younger, at times of an ephebe-like beauty, a man with barely any density, who danced across the stage like a golden-haired angel, a ghost. One of his Black musicians once said he was so white that he was transparent, even in the rock period there was something incredibly ephemeral about his appearance, as though each time he had once again freed himself from one of his made-up personas. He was then only what he wanted to be for other people, extremely desirable, at one of his performances women wanted to pull him from the stage, as if they might be able to tear him into pieces or rape him en masse, just as Orpheus was ripped apart by the Bacchantes, or as might happen when someone ventures too far into the myth that he himself created.

And Gombrowicz? Last year, in Zurich, I saw his *Yvonne, Princess of Burgundy*, one of those plays that, when you read it, you can scarcely believe, because how can the son of a king fall in love with a princess who is not only ugly as sin, but who also does not say a word, does not react even once, when the handsome young prince tells her that he wants to marry her? Gombrowicz apparently saw his play performed only once, in Paris. I saw it long after his death and wished he could have seen this performance, because everything that is strange and inaccessible about his work suddenly became clear and transparent. The play was performed solely by men, the queen mother was a transvestite taken to extremes, quite literally, as she was wearing an upright wig that went up half a metre into the air and moved like a vicious old queen according to all the clichés associated with the type.

But the beloved princess! Everything had been done to bring the utter absurdity to the fore. She looked like a Belgian butcher in a skimpy white communion dress, and the prince was truly in love with her. And what does all this have to do with David Bowie? In the few moments that Bowie spoke as himself in that film you could sense something of the ruthless game that was his life, a work of art upon which Gombrowicz could not have improved.

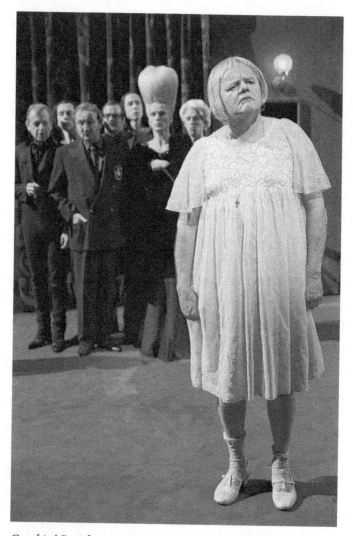

Gottfried Breitfuss as Yvonne, Princess of Burgundy.
Production by Barbara Frey, Schauspielhaus Zurich, 2015

77

Witchcraft. That was what I wanted to write about, but then my computer went haywire. We are not friends. Whenever my writing is going well, there are warnings of imminent danger, which I then ignore. This is followed by revenge – and not done by halves. The ragged ends of the lines that dominate the right-hand side of the page had leaped to the left, while you could have placed a ruler along the right: a bewitched page, which was in keeping with what I had wanted to write about. Far away on an island, I have no cavalry to call in at such moments, and when I tried it myself the devastating lightning struck and the whole page was gone, leaving behind a hole full of crushed and chewed-up words. The CD I had on was *Inferno* by Jan van Vlijmen, a dead composer who would not wish me any harm, so that could not be it. I tried to remember my lost words, but experience has taught me that the words I find will never be the same, vanished words are sacred words. For a moment I sit there, sinking into the sounds, sometimes vehement, of the *Inferno*, underrated music, played by the Schönberg Ensemble under Reinbert de Leeuw, and I thought about Jan van Vlijmen, whose house in Normandy I often visited, and also about the eight kilometres the composer covered on foot every day, there and back, to fetch his bread and newspaper in the neighbouring village. In the *Inferno*, the voices were travelling through high and inhospitable regions, but I could no longer bear to sit at the vengeful machine and I went outside. I still have my cactuses, who stand like loyal guards around the studio. The phallic one, always so green and rigidly upright, had stepped out of character and burst one of his seams, and it had been on my mind for a week. I had asked Xec about it, who said it didn't matter, he would heal himself. To find out what that torn wound felt like, I had laid my finger inside it and discovered that it contained a small green snail, or rather, that there was a very small snail in there, living inside a little snail shell in a thrilling shade of green. I eased it out of the elongated vertical wound with a stick and gently placed it on the damp soil. Fine, this is the day of witchcraft, because while I could still hear the *Inferno* playing inside, I saw that there was a small snail inside the wound again. The same one? These are mysteries that will never be solved here, it all counts as witchcraft, which is precisely what I had wanted to write about, because at this time of year Nature here is a little bewitched, grey skies and yet fields full of wild yellow flowers, raging wind and then a great silence again, as if nature is holding its breath. Yesterday I had driven to the other side of the island to visit one of the prehistoric monuments that are scattered over the islands, often constructions of stones so large that no human being could ever have lifted them, not even ten humans together, and yet that is exactly what they did. Winter is the best time for such expeditions, all the northerners have left, you are nearly always alone, a walker in a haunted landscape full of dead people about whom we know nothing. Son Catlar was the place I was on my way to. The first thing I encountered that day was an upside-down ship along the road to the capital, the Naveta des Tudons. In *naveta* there is the word "ship", and what you see is actually a sort of upturned ship of stone with a small opening at the western end through which, if you lie down on

Naveta des Tudons

your stomach, you can look inside. In this ship that is not a ship, people once laid their dead on the ground, sometimes with a jug or a piece of jewellery or another object beside them. They did not leave words behind, since they did not write. When the dead had decayed, the bones were removed from the skeleton and placed further away, to make room for other dead. I look into the empty, dark space, which smells of earth. The ship's walls slope upwards, the stones at the bottom are largest, in the distance the outlines of the mountains of Mallorca, which is where they came from, three thousand years ago. When I walk away and look back one last time, I see that ship lying there, silent and lonely in that landscape, a monument without any names.

Son Catlar is further to the south. I drive past a few isolated farmhouses, see hardly anyone, the wind makes the wild olive trees sway like drunken dancers, I see on the map that I have to look out for a farm called Egipte, it is supposed to be somewhere around there, not a *naveta* this time, but a *talayot*. Light grey, red and green are the predominant colours, the grey of the limestone rocks and the countless stone walls, the red of the earth, the green of the oleasters and the abundant vegetation. I leave the car in the empty carpark and walk towards a wall of gigantic stones. The book *Menorca Talayotica* says that it was the peasants of the island who gave the structures that name, no-one knows what name the people who built them gave to them. They would not have recognised the word *talayot*, and as I walk towards the wall, I think about how, where I am walking, a language was once spoken that has not only ceased to exist, but has not even left a trace, words vanished into the empty air. Just before the start of the wall, I see a deep cave, half hidden behind a tree. The sign beside it says it is a *hypogeum*, that the dead were buried in this cave, a thousand years before they were laid to rest in the *naveta*. I bend aside the branches of the tree and clamber over a few rocks into the depths, to the realm of the dead. When I am finally inside and my eyes are used to the darkness, I see that I am in a circular space. If there are any dead here, they must have turned to dust, they are silent, all I can hear is the trees outside. From the underworld I look out and see, by the light of the upper world, thistles and the yellow flowers that are called vinagrella here, but also dark-green, extremely vicious stinging nettles as the guardians of the dead and plants with tall, slender leaves, like a kind of wild leek. I try to pull one out of the ground, but it will not budge. In the summer I pick wild garlic like this, but this plant does not want to be picked. I break the stem and give it a try. It also tastes a lot like a leek. That evening we made a soup from it with a few vegetables and the nettles and the stalks of the vinagrella, which are like lemon.

From the guidebook I know that the wall around what was once a settlement is 876 metres in length, an elongated elliptical enclosure. Some of the stones are bigger than I am, here and there I see tumbledown towers of stones, sometimes it seems as if trees have grown straight through the stones, a marriage of old wood and limestone, twisted sculptures. There is a kind of gate, if I stoop I can enter. The remains of homes, then of a sort of sanctuary, late sunlight falls through the opening, I would like to hear singing, to see a fire. Who did they worship, who did they ask for protection? In the illustrations in *Menorca Talayotica*, someone has gone to town with people in animal skins, but I do not wish to have anything imposed on me. I want to imagine that I can hear voices, see fire, smell food. There are goats in those pictures, and goats have not changed their appearances or their voices, no more than the hawk I just spotted or the seagulls, who still use the same words. I read in the book that they had brought plants and animals with them, and in the all-encompassing silence I can imagine all kinds of things, a landing, a first night, the people eating the plants I just picked, but nothing of what you think is right and yet everything is right, the centuries it took them to build that wall of human-sized stones, the towers that served as signs to the outside, to the world, signs for others, to make a statement about the place they had founded, a boundary, a place where they were safe. I am alone and yet not alone, I walk the length of the entire wall and then again, seeing everything they saw and hearing the sound of their voices, watching as it slowly grows darker and then driving along narrow roads to the sea, which is close, and wild. The beach is covered with hairy balls of an incredibly fine fabric, a greeting from Poseidon. In the distance I see six or seven surfers riding the high waves, as if the waves are wild horses and the surfers the horsemen from some apocalypse or other, riders on horses made of water, from an age that no longer exists.

78

As I want to hear my news without advertisements, I listen to SWR2 in the morning at eight, a habit I developed in the months I spend every year in Baden-Württemberg. On the iPad, I can also listen to that same news in Amsterdam and on the Spanish island. What I like about it, apart from the absence of intrusive advertisements, is that SWR2 succeeds in moulding whatever has happened in the world into a perfectly measured time frame, as if the mixture of time and events were made of a special kind of clay. Disasters, bombings, sport, the stock exchange, the weather, China, refugees, executions, corruption, nothing ever lasts longer than ten minutes. You listen in the silence of your room to the daily summation of the world, but in fact I am always waiting for the last sentence with its laconic announcement: *Es ist acht Uhr zehn*. They have done it again, no disaster, no bombing, no beheading ever extends beyond those ten minutes, the cosmos is in order, you could place a metronome beside it.

Then come twenty just as perfectly balanced minutes, divided into three items, one times ten minutes and two times five minutes of current affairs, books or films, interviews. In my book *All Souls' Day*,[5] someone asks the sculptor, Victor, what he is doing in Germany. His answer is simple: "I like it there. Germans are so serious." That is probably why I listen to this broadcaster in the mornings, because every weekday, that half hour is followed by a programme that is announced with one single world: *Wissen*, and that does not mean "to

5 Translated into English by Susan Massotty.

delete, erase", as it does in Dutch, but "to know" or "know-ledge". I wait a moment to find out what it is about. I do not want to know everything, after all. But still, often enough I keep listening, and if it is particularly interesting you can download it for free, which is how, on September 14th, I found myself listening to a broadcast about the pensioners of space travel, and as so often happens I realised there was something I had never thought about. I already knew that *Voyager* had left the solar system – see 69 – and what was now happening or was going to happen, but I had never thought to wonder about the people who had worked on the project since the launch in 1977 or even before, as if those machines that were moving, so lonely, through that never entirely empty emptiness on their way to the nearest star or the Oort cloud or probably nothing else, had already cast off the people who had conceived them and taken care of them. Thanks to that broadcast, I made a few remarkable discoveries. Those people are still around, they still have names, and they follow the two Voyagers every day, perhaps because they are the only people who can operate the antiquated (!) equipment that is used to maintain contact. The electronics of the 1970s and the machine language of their ur-computer have become something solely for initiates. It sounded as if they had to make do with old coffee grinders and rubber bands, and there was a haze of melancholy and hopeless outdatedness over that whole programme, as if that group of lonely survivors were unable to abandon those two forsaken machines out there in infinity. And, in truth, they can't, because those eight people are the only ones who still understand the Voyagers' messages, and who can say what such a bond might mean after forty years? Each of the two machines is the size of a classic Volkswagen, crowned by an antenna of about three metres, aimed at the Earth, already billions of kilometres away. There was once a staff of two hundred, many of them have already been pensioned off, surplus to requirements. Others work part time at what sounds like an old clubhouse. When the Voyagers were still flying past planets, these people were indispensable, because they had to tell the probes by the second what to look at when making their recordings of those planets, which had never been seen in this way before, and the Earth dwellers watched with bated breath. Now there is nothing more to photograph, all that vast space looks the same, maybe it no longer matters where they are at which second, they are simply voyaging, trudging through measureless space until death comes. And still they have the same golden gramophone record (!) that Kurt Waldheim gave them in 1977, which no-one will ever listen to, even though it contains a thousand Lord's Prayers and Beethoven's Fifth and incomprehensible words in all the languages of the planet Earth, to which they will never return. That is perhaps our greatest hubris, that we believe there are beings like us out there. People who with their unimaginable hands (?) might unwrap that record and put it on a record player and hum along to the Fifth with tears in their impossible eyes (?) and long for us on our slowly dying star. To be on the safe side, a drawing was provided that shows how to build a record player. Perfect material for a comedy version of *Star Trek*.

*

Tom Weeks has been there since 1983. Five years before, he had seen *Star Wars* and knew at once where his calling lay. He is still responsible for keeping those two probes on course. At the time of the SWR2 broadcast, *Voyager 1* is flying north out of the solar system, with *Voyager 2* to the south of it, where there is still gravity, which *Voyager 1* has already left behind. And what is the probe doing out there? It is measuring the galactic wind. And number 2? It is also about to leave the solar system and, with it, the solar wind, probably in a year or two.

And Weeks himself? The broadcaster has a lot to say about him, mainly about his hair, a style known in German as the *Vokuhila*, which sounds to me like something from Hawaii. *Vorne kurz, hinten lang*, short at the front, long at the back, otherwise known as a mullet. I can picture it. Rock and roll was his first vocation, which was why he left Arizona for Los Angeles. He is a *shredder*, I can hear his electric guitar as he says the word. He would have liked to be on that record, along with Beethoven, but he did not make the cut. Out there, where no-one can hear anything, he cannot be heard either. He loves Eric Clapton and Jimi Hendrix. His desk is full of figures from *Star Wars* and *Star Trek* and his workspace is depicted as a children's room for grown-ups. And now? Now he takes care of the Voyagers because he never got a recording contract, even though he came close. It is NASA that has paid the bills, for all those years. And he is determined to stay with the Voyagers until the end. Perhaps he believes there are beings out there who will intercept the Voyagers and return them so that they can be displayed at the Smithsonian or its like.

Then I will have to rewrite *The Following Story*, I think, but I will not be part of the broadcast.

Tom Weeks's boss is Ed Stone, who is also his neighbour at work. His office is ten square metres and is located in Altadena, around a twenty-five minutes' drive from Pasadena, where the Jet Propulsion Laboratory is based, the centre where the most important space journeys are prepared and monitored, such as the journey to Mars. The Voyager mission was once housed there, but was later moved, as fewer people work on it. Stone is seventy-nine and has been there since the beginning, 1 July 1972. His workspace is not a children's room, Voyager is his life and will remain so. He tells his story: a student at the California Institute of Technology had, in 1965, discovered that all the outer planets, Jupiter, Saturn, Uranus and Neptune, would be aligned in 1977 – something that happens only once every 176 years. The problem was that spaceships back then lasted no longer than a year or two, so a mission that would take twelve years really was an impossibility. No-one could have known then that something could continue to exist in space for forty years. Space travel was only twenty years old at the time. Now we know better, and now Stone also wants to stay until the end, and by that he can only mean his own end, because there will be no end to the Voyagers, and for plans like that you need a special kind of patience, perhaps you have to be patience itself and not believe too much in your own mortality. Those last sentences are my own, because they do not say such things in Altadena. There, in the now of the radio programme, it is a Thursday morning and contact with

Voyager has been made, seventeen billion kilometres from the Earth and therefore seventeen hours in the past, because that is how long it takes for the data to reach Earth. The three control stations have received them and sent them to those few old buildings: diagrams and tables that allow the team to see that everything is working and in good shape, including *Voyager* itself. The data are studied by scientists all over America, the magnetic field, the cosmic radiation. Two or three times a year, they all come together at the Space Vatican, the Jet Propulsion Laboratory, to compare everything and decide what to publish.

Suzanne Dodd has been there for thirty-two years and remembers the time when they flew past the planets, the negotiations about which instrument should be aimed at which part of the planet, because everyone had a different task, and time was precious. Who does what? Every instrument wants to probe in a different direction at the same time. There were eleven instruments on board. So, it was about negotiation, haggling, letting others take priority, shifting something to five hours later, and all with the utmost precision. That took years, until they had passed all the planets, because after Neptune there was nothing. We no longer photograph anything, and the cameras no longer do anything.

And so the Voyagers continue with their eyes closed, racing through the universe as blind as bats. There is nothing left to photograph. What they are still doing is measuring the magnetic fields out there and the strength and direction of the radiation from high-energy particles. That does give us some kind of picture of the interstellar environment that the *Voyager* is traversing. "Environment"! All we have are the words we have. I try, here on my island, to imagine an environment of billions of square kilometres, but I cannot do it.

Suzanne Dodd can, though. She can see the future clearly. The *Voyager* is a nuclear-power plant, she says, one that's losing four watts a year. By 2020, they will have switched off the instruments. By 2025, they won't have enough power to run the scientific equipment. After that, they'll only be able to receive technical details about the flight until 2030. But no-one wants to break the connection. They've disabled just about all the instruments they can. It's incredibly cold out there, and they can't turn off anything that might freeze the propellant pipes, because then the probe will no longer be able to point its antenna at Earth, and that would be the end of all their work. Dodd says that they are all too old to find another job.

The two Voyagers will fly on, no matter what happens to the people down below – another meaningless term. They will have died a hundred times by the time *Voyager 1*, forty thousand years from now, blind and silent, comes in the vicinity of a star, but vicinity, too, is a word without terrestrial meaning, because *Voyager* will never come as close to that star as it is now to the sun. The planets and the sun are miserable little villages in the empty cosmos. The star that *Voyager*, with its golden gramophone record, will fly past in forty thousand years' time has a fitting name: AC+793888, there is nothing human about it, even though AC+ does live in the constellation of Ursa Minor, the Little Bear.

And pausing to say hello is not an option either: every day, *Voyager* travels one and a half million kilometres, four times the distance from Earth to the Moon. St Jerome had a skull on his desk to remind him of the vanity of existence. The *Voyager* will circle the centre of the Milky Way for ever (?), no-one can do anything to change that now. Or as Herman Mussert puts it in *The Following Story*: "By that time the ashes of the ashes of our ashes would long since have disowned our provenance", but that is not how they think about it there in Altadena. There, ash is just ash, and saints and their skulls belong in the church. Ed Stone says that what they did was send a message to everyone – that it was possible. Maybe I prefer to stay closer to Borges, who felt a sense of hilarity at all these puzzles, and I can define that only as the elation that a thousand elegant question marks without a lasting answer can bring. The next destination of the Voyagers is a Dutch province, in three hundred years' time they will be at the innermost edge of the Oort cloud, an inhospitable gathering point for comets, gas, trillions of chunks of ice and pieces of rock, to which the Dutch astronomer Jan Hendrik Oort gave his name. The distances there are measured in numbers I cannot pronounce, here even Lucebert's breadcrumb becomes invisible ("the awareness / of being a breadcrumb on the skirt of the universe"). I head outside to look at my part of the universe. Because what is the difference, actually? The Voyagers are there, and I am here, also in space, and I too am apparently going somewhere at great speed. I remember the LSD guru Timothy Leary, who decided that after his death his ashes would be shot two hundred kilometres into space in a rocket. Then he would be *there*. But where? He really had not grasped it at all. Given the distances we are talking about, he would have been nowhere then, or in other words simply here, where I am, also in space, but two hundred kilometres away. Space is all around. Those beings for whom that golden record was intended are ourselves. We are the only ones in the neighbourhood. Are we all alone? Yes, until further notice. Tonight a programme with three Dutch politicians, about a possible journey to Mars in 2050. That journey will last almost a year, I do not know if that was mentioned in the programme. Almost an entire year with just a few people in a limited space. Then you're there, in our newest colony. Don't forget to take the flag, say goodbye for ever, because those who go will probably never return.

79

It is a bright January day. The cactus with the wicked weapons has extremely small yellow flowers, the small downy cactuses in their pots have the same in purple, and there are hundreds of buds and the first white blossoms on the ancient almond tree, which has been sawn in half. I decide that the cosmos is an illusion, and I feel the urge to kiss the soil of my garden, like a Polish pope.

80

Evening and farewell, as always. Tomorrow *tramontana*, a storm from the north, but now the sky is still clear. I drive to Punta Prima to look at the lighthouse on the Isla del Aire, the Island of the Air, the island of thistles and black lizards, a land without people. The sea here moves differently, has time to think. Between the Middle Ages and modern times, hundreds of ships have perished around these shores, they rock gently down there with their dead. *Shipwreck with Spectator* is the name of a book by Hans Blumenberg. People who witness a shipwreck stand on the shore, unable to help. He has gathered metaphors about ships and transience, Lucretius, Virgil, Nietzsche, Schopenhauer, the sea and uncertainty, the fates of people. I stand very still for a time, the mechanical light in the distance follows its own electrical laws, an irregular but calculated heartbeat, on-off, on-off, waiting, then full on again, for a moment it shines like white chalk across the ink-black water, as bright as Sirius at the feet of Orion. Last week a yacht went down, a man overboard, his body found with shark bites. I think of the two Voyagers in their waterless ocean, beyond the domain of the sun on their way to a cloud full of dangers, on their way to the everywhere of the cosmic void, to the home of the following star.

San Luis – Hofgut Missen – San Luis,
1 August 2014–5 January 2016

The following works have been quoted from or paraphrased in *533 Days*:

Das Buch gegen den Tod, Elias Canetti (München: Hanser Verlag, 2014)

Diary by Witold Gombrowicz, translated from the Polish by Lillian Vallee (New Haven and London: Yale University Press/Margellos Republic of Letters, 2012)

Cosmos by Witold Gombrowicz, translated from the Polish by Danuta Borchardt (New York: Grove Press, 2011)

Excerpt of *Oblivion* by Héctor Abad, translated from the Spanish by Anne McLean and Rosalind Harvey. English translation originally published in 2010 by Old Street Publishing, Ltd., Great Britain. Published in the United States in 2012 by Farrar, Straus, and Giroux. Copyright 2006 by Héctor Abad. Translation copyright 2010 by Anne McLean and Rosalind Harvey. Originally published in Spanish by Planeta, Spain, as *El olvido que seremos* in 2006.

Towards the One & Only Metaphor by Miklós Szentkuthy, translated from the Hungarian by Tim Wilkinson (New York & Berlin: Contra Mundum Press, 2013)

Tagebuch 1966–1971 by Max Frisch (Frankfurt am Main: Suhrkamp, 1972) in Laura Watkinson's translation from the German

The Following Story by Cees Nooteboom in Ina Rilke's translation from the Dutch (London: Harvill Press, 1994)

Tage mit Gombrowicz by István Eörsi (Leipzig: Gustav Kiepenheuer, 1997)

CEES NOOTEBOOM was born in 1933 in The Hague. His first novel, *Philip and the Others*, appeared in 1955, and since then he has built up an impressive oeuvre of novels, poetry, short stories and travelogues. His work has earned him numerous awards, including the Bordewijk Prize and the (American) Pegasus Prize for *Rituals* (1980), and the Aristeion European Prize for Literature for *The Following Story* (1991). The latter has been translated into more than twenty languages and signalled his international breakthrough. In 2004 he was awarded the prestigious P. C. Hooft Prize for his entire oeuvre. Among his other books are the novels *In the Dutch Mountains* (1984), *All Souls' Day* (1998) and *Lost Paradise* (2004). His travelogues include *Roads to Santiago* (1992), *Roads to Berlin* (2009), which won him the German 3rd of October Literature Prize, and *Venice* (2020). Together with his wife, the photographer Simone Sassen, he has also created an illustrated work *Tumbas*, on the graves of writers, philosophers and poets. He lives between Amsterdam, the island of Menorca (also the inspiration for another of his works of non-fiction, *Letters to Poseidon*), and southern Germany.

LAURA WATKINSON lived in England, Scotland, Italy and Germany, before settling in the Netherlands in 2003. Her previous translations include Cees Nooteboom's *Roads to Berlin*, *Letters to Poseidon* and *Venice*, Peter Terrin's *Post Mortem*, Otto de Kat's *The Longest Night* and *Freetown*, and Tonke Dragt's *The Letter for the King*.